THE JOSEPH ANOINTING

LIVING ABOVE THE SUN

Unlocking Your Destiny in
Times of Testing and Promotion

ERIC COOPER

THE JOSEPH ANOINTING

LIVING ABOVE THE SUN

Unlocking Your Destiny in Times of Testing and Promotion

ISBN (Paperback Print Edition): 978-1-0688200-1-4
ISBN (eBook Edition): 978-1-0688200-2-1
ISBN (Hardcover Print Edition): 9798289950765

To inquire about speaking engagements, bulk orders, or media requests, please contact: contact@abovethesun.ca

www.abovethesun.ca

Book design and cover design by:
Above the Sun Consultant Group Inc.
First Edition: September 2025

ABOVE THE SUN
CONSULTANT GROUP

Scripture Permissions:

DEDICATION

To the dreamers.

To those who have walked through fire with nothing but a whisper from God.

To the misunderstood, the misjudged, the hidden— not because you lacked value, but because Heaven was guarding your unveiling.

To the sons and daughters of Yahweh who have chosen the pit over compromise, the prison over bitterness, and the palace—not for pride, but as a place of provision and purpose.

You are not forgotten.

You are being revealed.

For such a time as this, the anointing upon your life is rising— and the world will see what God has been forming in secret.

What People Are Saying...

"A life-changing and eye-opening book."

"This book had a profound impact on me. It's incredibly relatable—addressing real problems, offering practical solutions, and releasing powerful, prophetic prayers. What sets it apart is its universal message of forgiveness and healing. I've even shared photos of the pages that touched me most, hoping others will be inspired as well." — Sylvia, Verified Amazon Review (Canada)

"Solid biblically and applicable too!"

"Many books share the 'what'—but not the 'how.' Not this book. It's grounded in truth and full of practical wisdom." — Kevin T., Verified Amazon Review (United States)

"Reading chapter one fueled a fire..."

"This book speaks to the dreamer in me—the one who used to wonder if dreams were selfish, or sacred. It stirred something deep. Our dreams matter to God. And this book reminds me to dream again." — Reid T., Early Reader

PREFACE

There's a reason this book found its way into your hands. Like Joseph, you may have walked through seasons that didn't make sense— when dreams felt too distant, when the pit felt more real than the promise.

I know that feeling.

This book was not written from a platform—it was born in the quiet spaces between heartbreak from others' betrayal and God's healing, between loss and revelation, between the silence of waiting and the voice of God.

Each chapter is more than teaching—it's testimony.

More than revelation—it's remembrance.

It carries the sound of surrender, the weight of process, and the hope of restoration.

I believe Yahweh is ready to stir something deep within you as you read—to unlock the Joseph anointing that has been waiting for its time.

May these words serve as both a mirror to your calling and a map for your journey.
Because you weren't just born for survival.
You were born to reign—*above the sun.*

The Joseph Anointing:
Living Above the Sun

A Prophetic Journey into Identity, Process, and Reformation

- What if your delays were divine?
- What if your betrayals were birthing something bigger than you imagined?
- What if your hidden years were preparation for global impact?

The Joseph Anointing: Living Above the Sun unlocks the ancient, unfolding story of Joseph—not as a distant biblical figure, but as a divine blueprint for those walking through the fire of preparation in this generation.

This is not just a teaching—it's a *prophetic commissioning* for the misjudged, the hidden, and the hopeful. It's a call to rise from the pit, endure the prison, and step boldly into the palace—not for pride, but for purpose.

Drawn from scripture, personal testimony, and spiritual insight, *The Joseph Anointing* reveals how Yahweh uses the very things meant to break us—to build us. You'll gain clarity on the unique process that forges true spiritual authority and unlocks reformation.

In these pages, you'll discover:

- How to carry a prophetic dream without being destroyed by delay
- How to walk in sonship, integrity, and forgiveness—no matter the betrayal
- Why Joseph's story is a prophetic template for modern-day reformers
- What it means to *live above the sun* and reign from the secret place
- The six prophetic pillars of the Joseph anointing—and how to walk them out
- How God uses obscurity, misunderstanding, and pain to birth legacy

Whether you are in a season of waiting, rebuilding, or stepping into leadership, this book will *realign your vision, reignite your hope, and reposition you for destiny.*

You are not forgotten. You are not disqualified.

You are the fulfillment of the dream.

ACKNOWLEDGMENTS

I give all glory to **Yahweh**—my Creator, my Father, my King.

Thank You for shaping me in the secret place, for holding me through every storm, and for teaching me to live not under the sun—but above it.

To **Holy Spirit**—my closest Friend and infinite Wisdom. You are the whisper that steadies my soul and the wind that carries me higher. You have never left me.

To **my children**—your lives are arrows in the hands of a faithful God. I love you all, and I remain expectant for all that you will become.

To **my grandchildren**—you are my crown of legacy and the reason I continue to write, pray, and believe.

To **my family**, and to those whose reconciliation is still unfolding—thank you for being part of my story.
I hold space for grace, always.

To **Kevin Thompson**—you have walked with me through fire and into the future. You see the unseen. The road ahead is radiant, and we've only just begun.

To **every reader**— Thank you for opening your heart to this message. You're not just reading a testimony—you are stepping into your own Joseph journey. And I pray that what Yahweh did for me, He now begins in you.

Contents

Introduction 1

Section I – The Forming 5
Chapter 1: Dreamer, Son, Reformer................5

Chapter 2: The Joseph Effect..........................13

Chapter 3: Living Above the Sun 19

Section II – The Breaking 29
Chapter 4: The Pit and the Process 29

Chapter 5: Legacy of Forgiveness 51

Chapter 6: Forgiveness and the Family Line...61

Chapter 7: Cancelled But Not Conquered 73

Section III – The Rising....................................91
Chapter 8: Reigning with Wisdom 91

Chapter 9: The Storehouse Anointing 103

Chapter 10: Above the Sun: Reigning from the Mountain Now 111

Chapter 11: The Anointing That Abides 117

Conclusion: You Are the Fulfillment of the Dream..125

The Six Prophetic Pillars of the....................129

Joseph Anointing 129

Appendix: Deeper Reflections........................133
Scriptural Bibliography 142

About The Author...151
Books by Eric D. Cooper.................................153

The Joseph Anointing

From my earliest memories, I've been a dreamer.

Even before I understood the language of the Spirit, I carried an awareness of something greater—something above and beyond what my eyes could see.

I dreamed of purpose, of people being healed, of nations turning back to God. I didn't know then that these dreams weren't just my imagination— they were the whispers of Heaven calling me into identity.

For as long as I can remember, I've related to the story of Joseph. Not as a distant biblical character, but as a living pattern that mirrored my own life.

Like Joseph, I was misunderstood and mislabeled. I experienced favor, then was forgotten. I was promoted—and then stripped of what I thought would last. But through it all, *the Lord never left me.*

The path of Joseph is not for the faint of heart. It is the path of refinement, of surrender, and ultimately, of reformation. Joseph's life prophesies the rise of a generation who will walk in wisdom, authority, and mercy—not to build monuments to themselves, but to build storehouses of provision and healing for others.

This book is not just about Joseph—*it's about you.* It's about the *sons and daughters of Yahweh* who are being called out of obscurity and into destiny. It's about the dreamers who have been rejected, the reformers who have been tested, and the leaders who have been hidden—for such a time as this.

The ***Joseph Anointing*** is a Kingdom mantle for this generation. It's the call to live *above the sun*, to see from Heaven's perspective, and to operate in the authority of *sons and daughters seated with Christ in Heavenly places.* It is a call to maturity, to forgiveness, to innovation, and to legacy.

As you read this book, my prayer is that you don't just gain insight—*you gain identity*. That you don't just read my story—*you awaken to your own*. Because the same God who was with Joseph in the pit, the prison, and the palace—*is with you.*

May this book ignite the blueprint within you. May it call forth the reformer in you. And may it remind you that your greatest authority won't come from what you build—but from what you surrender.

Welcome to the mountain.

Welcome to the place *above the sun.*

—Eric

A Note on Terminology

Throughout this book, you'll notice I refer to God as *Yahweh*—the sacred and covenantal name revealed in Scripture. This is a personal choice, rooted in reverence and relationship. I also speak of *Holy Spirit* as a Person, capitalized in full, to reflect *His Divine* nature and nearness in my life.

I also use the terms *"sons"* and *"sonship"* to describe our identity as *God's children*, drawing from Galatians 3:26-28, where Paul calls believers *"sons of God"* through faith in Christ. In this biblical context, *"sons"* (*Greek:huioi*) signifies the full rights and intimacy of adoption into God's family, available to all—*male and female* alike—for *"there is neither male nor female"* in Christ. This language reflects the privilege of inheritance and purpose, inviting every reader to embrace their identity as a beloved heir, united in God's redemptive plan.

These choices are intentional. They reflect not just theology, *but intimacy.* My prayer is that, as you read, these names and terms would draw you closer to the heart of *the One* who gave them, awakening you to your calling to *live above the sun.*

Introduction

The Promises Are Alive

For most of my life, I've felt a deep connection to the story of Joseph—not just as a biblical figure, but as a prophetic reflection of my own journey. Like Joseph, I've been a dreamer since childhood. I've seen things before they happened. I've sensed the pull of a future reality even while walking through the pain of the present. And like Joseph, I've walked through betrayal, misunderstanding, rejection, and long seasons of hiddenness.

As a young boy, I faced labels, bullying, and misunderstanding from those who couldn't see what God had placed within me. I built walls to survive, forged in rejection's fire, feeling at times like I was thrown into a pit. Yet even there, Yahweh's presence surrounded me, shaping me for a purpose greater than my pain.

Yet through every chapter of my life, the Lord remained faithful. His presence never left me. Even in my hidden seasons, His hand was shaping me. I've experienced great favor and endured deep loss. I've been raised up—and brought low. But I've come to learn this: the promises of God are not fragile. They are fire-tested. They do not evaporate in seasons of trial—they are proven in them.

Recently, the Lord began leading me to study His promises to Joseph more deeply. As I obeyed, I began to see more than a Bible study—I saw a map. A divine blueprint. A prophetic pattern not just for my life, but for the sons and daughters of Yahweh in this generation. *This book is the fruit of that encounter.*

In these pages, I will walk with you through what I call *The Joseph Anointing—Six Prophetic pillars* drawn from Joseph's life. This book unveils six prophetic pillars—*Dreamer, Son, Servant, Prisoner, Prophet, Governor*—guiding you from the pit to the palace. These pillars are not formulas; they are formation. They speak to identity, pain, process, promotion, and purpose. They are meant to awaken the Joseph inside of you.

I am a spiritual being, that has a soul, that lives in a body. My spirit is possessed by Holy Spirit. I live more in the spiritual realm of Yahweh than in the natural realm beneath the sun. I live *above the sun.*

This is not poetry—it is my posture. I write from a place of Kingdom alignment. I do not wait for Heaven. I live from it. I do not walk as a servant— I walk as a son. And I believe with all my heart that this generation is not waiting for another preacher... it's groaning for the revealing of the sons of God (*Romans 8:19*).

My heart is to see you walk in your prophetic identity. To see you forgive like Joseph, rule like Joseph, weep like Joseph, build like Joseph—and ultimately, to prepare the way for others, just as Joseph did.

Your journey matters. Your scars are sacred. Your dreams carry divine blueprints. And these promises—they are alive... and they are for you, too.

"Your eyes saw my unformed body; all the days ordained for me were written in Your book before one of them came to be." —Psalm 139:16

The Cost of the Anointing

When you truly invite Holy Spirit into your life, you're not asking for comfort—you're asking for consecration. You're yielding to a fire that does not flatter, but refines (Malachi 3:2-3). His guidance will not simply lead you—it will undo you. The ego must die, pride must fall, and every false identity must be stripped away (Galatians 2:20). But in that holy death, resurrection power is released (Romans 8:11). What rises is not just a better version of you—it is Christ in you, the hope of glory (Colossians 1:27). This is not mere direction—it is divine possession. And it changes everything.

There's a hidden cost to the anointing—one few speak of, but every chosen one eventually learns. To walk in divine purpose is to embrace a path that will break you before it builds you. Joseph didn't just wear a coat of many colors; he wore a mantle that would cost him everything.

This is the journey Joseph walked. This is the call on every dreamer marked by heaven. Not just to be seen—but to be sifted (Luke 22:31-32). Not just to rule—but to serve (Matthew 23:11). Not just to interpret dreams—but to survive the pit that prepares you to fulfill them (Genesis 50:20).

Section I – The Forming
Chapter 1: Dreamer, Son, Reformer

"Then Joseph had a dream..." —Genesis 37:5

From the beginning, Joseph was marked by dreams. Not ambition. Not manipulation. Not striving. Dreams.

They came uninvited, yet undeniable—*whispers of eternity breaking into time.* And like Joseph, I didn't ask to be a dreamer. I simply was one.

As a child, I saw things others didn't. I would sit alone for hours, not out of loneliness, but because I felt something more—*a pull from beyond the veil.* I didn't have the words for it then, but I know now: *it was the Spirit of Yahweh stirring the eternal within me.*

I wasn't raised to chase platforms or power. I was raised to seek the presence of God. Even before I knew what ministry was, I was already walking with Him. I didn't know I was prophetic. I just thought I was different. That difference, however, made me a target.

Like Joseph, I faced misunderstanding and isolation, often feeling thrown into pits not of my making. Yet these moments, though painful, marked me for a divine purpose, shaping me as a dreamer under Yahweh's hand.

And yet... I never stopped dreaming.

The Dreamer

Dreams are often the first language of destiny. They come when you're too young to earn them and too naïve to fear them. When Joseph dreamed of the stars and the sheaves, he had no idea that his dream would require betrayal, slavery, and prison before it would produce harvest.

I still remember one of the first dreams I ever dared to speak aloud. I was just a teenager—full of faith, full of fire—and I shared with someone close to me that I was going to build a house. Not someday. Not theoretically. I told her I was going to build it in the garage behind my family home.

It wasn't a metaphor. It wasn't a grand spiritual analogy. It was a real vision I had—clear, vivid, and alive inside me. The only problem was, I had no framework for what I was actually seeing. I thought it meant now. I didn't yet understand that some dreams are glimpses into the future— not instructions for the present.

So I spoke it boldly. Naively. And she laughed.

My friend at the time didn't just question it—she dismissed it. As if I were making it up, exaggerating, or playing some kind of fantasy game. That laughter? It pierced. It left a mark. Not because she didn't believe in my abilities, but because she didn't see what I saw.

That moment—small as it might seem—was one of the first times I tasted the cost of being a dreamer. I learned something Joseph knew all too well: not everyone can handle the vision God plants in your heart. Especially when it doesn't fit the timeline or logic of this world.

But I also learned this: just because a dream seems delayed, doesn't mean it's denied. Sometimes, what looks like a garage is really the blueprint for a house. And sometimes, what feels like rejection is really God refining your clarity.

And I had no idea that the dreams God gave me would be tested in the same way.

"Until the time that His word came to pass, the word of the Lord tested him." —Psalm 105:19

That verse has lived in my bones. Because like Joseph, my calling was confirmed not in comfort, but in contradiction. My dreams were not destroyed—they were refined.

The Son

What sustained Joseph wasn't just the dream—it was his identity. He knew who he was: **a son.** Even when stripped of his coat, sold by his brothers, and forgotten in prison, he never forgot whose he was.

I've learned that the power of sonship is not found in the approval of people—*it's found in the presence of the Father*. In my darkest moments, when all seemed lost, it wasn't a title or a ministry that held me—it was the whisper of the Father saying, ***"You are still Mine."***

Sonship is the soil from which Kingdom authority grows. Servants labor for favor, but *sons labor from favor*. Joseph didn't manipulate his way to the throne—*he interpreted his way there*. His posture as a son gave him *eyes to see and ears to hear* what others could not.

The Reformer

Joseph's dream wasn't about fame—*it was about famine.* He was raised up, not just to interpret dreams, *but to reform a nation.* To build storehouses. To preserve life. To become a solution in a time of shaking.

This is the pattern I've seen in my own life. Every loss has become a blueprint. Every scar, a strategy. I am not called to build an empire—*I am called to help build Goshen—***places of refuge, revelation, and reformation.**

Joseph was not just a ruler. He was a reconciler. A provider. A bridge between generations. And this is the anointing being released in our time: *dreamers who build, sons who govern, reformers who reconcile.*

A Word from My Heart to Yours

Friend, if you're anything like me, you've probably carried dreams that once felt alive—only to see them buried by disappointment. Maybe life happened. Maybe betrayal hit. Maybe time passed, and you started wondering if you missed it.

I want to say this: **You didn't miss it.**

What God authored in you is not fragile. It's fire-tested. Ask Holy Spirit to breathe on what looks buried. He's not done yet.

And can I ask you something gently—but boldly?

Are you living like a servant trying to earn approval, or like a son or daughter who already has it?

You were never meant to strive for validation.

You were created to move from the Father's affirmation.

Let Him whisper again: *You are Mine.*

I'm proud of you.

Also—don't underestimate what you've been called to build.

There are people, systems, and family lines that need the blueprint you carry.

You're not just here to prophesy to dry bones. You're called to build what lives after resurrection. That's legacy. That's reformation.

I see you. More importantly, He *sees you.*

Prophetic Declaration

I am a dreamer, called by God before I was formed.

I am a son, sealed by the Spirit of adoption.

I am a reformer, positioned in this generation for such a time as this.

I will not despise the pit—I will trust the process.

I live above the sun, from Heaven's perspective.

The dreams of my youth are not fantasy—they are prophecy.

And they shall come to pass.

Chapter 2: The Joseph Effect

— A Prophetic Blueprint for the Sons of God

> *"Go and see about the welfare of your brothers and the welfare of the flock, and bring word back to me." —Genesis 37:14*

Joseph didn't go looking for greatness. He went looking for his brothers.

And that, right there, is the beginning of the Joseph effect. The call wasn't about ego—it was about obedience. His journey didn't begin with a throne. It began with a commission from his father.

The Joseph Effect is what happens when a son says yes—not to position, but to purpose. It's what happens when someone carries a Kingdom dream through the pit, the prison, and into the palace—not for self-preservation, but to preserve a people.

A Prophetic Pattern in Scripture

From Genesis to Revelation, God often hides His blueprints in people. Joseph's life wasn't just a story—it was a shadow of the coming Son. He was betrayed by his own, thrown into a pit, sold for silver, falsely accused, forgotten... and then, in the fullness of time, raised up to bring life to nations.

He became a type and shadow of Jesus:

- A son sent by his father

- Rejected by his own

- Elevated to save both Jew and Gentile

- A reconciler of generations

- A preserver of promise

This is the Joseph Effect: a prophetic blueprint for all who carry the Spirit of Christ. And it is more relevant today than ever before.

The Sons Must Arise

"For the creation waits in eager expectation for the revealing of the sons of God." —Romans 8:19

The world is not waiting for another celebrity pastor. It's groaning for the rise of true sons—those who have been formed in the fire, refined in the prison, and elevated in secret.

Joseph did not run a campaign to become Prime Minister of Egypt. He was pulled out of prison at the exact time the world was starving for wisdom. Heaven's promotion always aligns with Earth's hunger.

And this is why you've been hidden, misunderstood, processed, and preserved. Because you are not just carrying a gift—*you are carrying a blueprint.*

You are part of this Joseph generation.

Carriers of Strategy, Forgiveness, and Legacy

Joseph carried what his generation needed—but they didn't recognize it at first. Neither will you always be recognized for what you carry. But your authority doesn't come from visibility. It comes from alignment.

Joseph didn't just interpret dreams—he translated the wisdom of God into systems, strategies, and solutions. He didn't just weep in private—he forgave in public. He didn't just save a nation—he secured a legacy that would point forward to the Messiah.

This is your invitation.

You are not just called to dream. You are called to build, forgive, restore, and govern. This is the Joseph Effect: not just survival, but strategic sonship for the sake of generations.

Can I speak to the part of you that's been hidden for a long time—the part that's been processed in secret, in silence, maybe even in pain?

I know what it's like to wonder if the delay was divine or just disappointing.

But I promise you this: *Heaven sees what no one else applauds.*

That quiet obedience?

That unseen surrender?

It's not wasted. It's preparation for something far greater than you imagined. Ask Holy Spirit to show you how this hiddenness has aligned you for impact.

And let's talk about the pit. I know it's real. I've been there too. But here's what I've learned: the pit doesn't cancel the promise—it shapes the vessel who will carry it. Don't fixate on the pain. Let God reframe it. There's a palace on the other side, and your perspective will determine how you carry what's coming.

Lastly, I want to ask you something tender but weighty: *Is there someone you're being called to forgive or reconcile with—not because it's easy, but because it's eternal?* Legacy doesn't come through revenge. It comes through release. And sometimes, the most powerful healing you'll ever offer is a quiet yes to forgiveness.

Your story matters. And it's not over.

Prophetic Declaration

I am not chasing position—I am stewarding purpose.

I am a son, sent by the Father, refined for this generation.

I will carry Heaven's blueprint into Earth's famine.

I choose legacy over recognition, obedience over fame.

I forgive, I restore, I lead with mercy.

I walk in the Joseph effect.

And I will not waste my pain.

Chapter 3: Living Above the Sun

— *A Kingdom Mindset Rooted in Eternity*

"Set your mind on things above, not on things on the earth. For you died, and your life is hidden with Christ in God." —Colossians 3:2–3

To live above the sun is to live from another realm.

It's not poetic—*it's prophetic*. It's not future tense—*it's now*. As *sons and daughters* of Yahweh, we are not called to merely survive this life—we are called to rule and reign with Christ from the realm we were born of: *the Spirit*.

For years, I related to Joseph as a dreamer. But what truly set him apart was not just his gift—it was his perspective. In every chapter of his story, Joseph chose to see from above the pain, the betrayal, the delay. He saw beyond what was happening to him and into what God was doing through him.

That's what it means to live *above the sun*.

When Offense Was a Choice, but Heaven Was My Home

There came a moment—one marked by real pain—when I could have chosen offense. I had been misunderstood, spoken about in ways that didn't reflect my heart, and deeply wounded in a place where I had given much.

The temptation to defend myself, to speak up, to set the record straight was strong. I wrestled with it—truly, I did. But in that tension, Holy Spirit whispered a higher call: *"Live above the sun."* Not every injustice requires retaliation. Sometimes, the greatest victory is found in quiet surrender to Heaven's perspective.

I knew in that moment I was being invited to respond from the realm I was born of, not the one I was attacked in. So, I stayed quiet. I chose forgiveness. I let God be my Defender. And something broke—not just around me, but in me.

 The desire to be understood was swallowed up by the peace of being hidden in Christ. I've come to realize this: offense is the language of those still living under the sun. But those who live from above walk in mercy, silence, and wisdom. I didn't lose that battle—I won it by surrender.

A Life Hidden in Christ

Paul's letter to the Colossians reminds us that our true life is *"hidden with Christ in God."* That's not just positional theology—*it's practical spiritual reality.*

Joseph's ability to interpret dreams, to resist bitterness, to walk in wisdom—all flowed from a hidden place. He wasn't led by offense—*he was led by insight.*

Living *above the sun* means walking in Kingdom awareness even when the pit is deep, the prison is long, and the promise feels distant.

It means knowing that Heaven holds your coordinates— even when Earth mislabels your location.

You may be in a pit—*but you're not forgotten.* You may be hidden—*but you're not buried.* You may be stripped—*but you're not empty.*

You are hidden in Christ—and He is always seen.

A Spiritual Being First

"In Him we live and move and have our being."
—Acts 17:28

This truth has become a cornerstone for me: *I am a spiritual being, that has a soul, that lives in a body. My spirit is possessed by Holy Spirit.* I do not live under the sun, dictated by what I see—I live above it, *governed by Who I know.*

This is not escapism. This is spiritual government. Joseph governed Egypt not by natural means, but by divine discernment. Likewise, you have access to wisdom, revelation, and strategy that can only be received from above.

To walk in *the Joseph Anointing*, you must first *reclaim your heavenly seat.* You are not trying to get to Heaven—*you're learning to live from it.*

Mindset Precedes Manifestation

Before Joseph ever ruled in Egypt, he reigned in his mindset. He reigned over bitterness. Over despair. Over vengeance. He lived like a son even while wearing the clothes of a slave.

This Kingdom mindset is not a motivational slogan—*it's a spiritual alignment.* It's setting your mind *above the sun*, where the will of the Father flows uninterrupted. *It's viewing your life through the eyes of Heaven, not the lens of trauma.*

The Josephs of this generation are being raised up to interpret the times, but first we must learn to interpret our own trials.

Your pit is not a grave— *it's a proving ground.* Your prison is not punishment—*it's preparation.*

When you live *above the sun*, you see every delay as divine. Every loss as redirection. Every betrayal as a setup for breakthrough.

Servant: Humility in Hiddenness

Before Joseph ever stood before Pharaoh, he served in silence. He labored in Potiphar's house— faithful with what wasn't his, diligent with no audience, righteous when no reward followed.

This is the hidden pillar of the Joseph Anointing: *the call to serve when no one sees you.*

Some of my most formative years were spent in this quiet place—serving others, supporting visions not my own, and laying bricks no one noticed.

I didn't understand it then, but the posture of a servant became the proving ground for my future authority.

When you embrace servanthood without striving for visibility, Heaven begins to trust you with influence.

You learn to lead by lifting, to follow without frustration, and to sow without demanding harvest. And this is how kings are trained—in obscurity, not on platforms.

Joseph learned to manage a household before he managed a nation.

You must first serve faithfully what belongs to another before you can steward what belongs to you (Luke 16:12).

Hebraic Insights: Joseph's Perspective

Dr. Eli Lizorkin-Eyzenberg, in *The Hebrew Story of Joseph*, emphasizes the depth of Joseph's character and the nuances often lost in translation. He notes:

"Joseph goes from Hebrew slave to Vizier of Egypt and savior of his family. He lays aside resentment and offers forgiveness and reconciliation."

This perspective aligns with the Kingdom mindset we're exploring.

Joseph's ability to forgive and reconcile wasn't just a personal virtue—it was a manifestation of living above the sun, seeing God's greater plan amidst personal trials.

Let Me Talk to You for a Moment...

You may have found yourself in a situation recently where offense was knocking at the door— maybe even banging. Maybe you were overlooked, misunderstood, or falsely accused. I know those moments well. But here's the question I want to ask you: *Did you choose offense... or did you choose elevation?* Did you respond from the natural or rise into the spiritual? Be honest with yourself. Ask Holy Spirit to show you what governed your response—and let Him refine your reflex.

Now take a moment to reflect on this: *What does it mean for you to be hidden in Christ right now?* Not in theory, but in this season. Is He shielding you? Preserving you? Preparing you? Write it down. Let it become your anchor.

And finally, where in your life are you still living *"under the sun"*—reacting to pressure, people, or problems instead of responding from your seat in heavenly places? Identify it. Name it. Then declare Heaven's perspective over that area. Because you don't belong under the weight—you were born to rule above it.

Prophetic Declaration and Prayer of Alignment

As you journey through the lessons of this chapter, you've been invited to live above the sun, to rise above the weight of offense and the clamor of earthly pressures.

Like Joseph, who carried a Kingdom mindset through the pain of misunderstanding, you are called to anchor your identity in Heaven's truth, not the world's accusations.

This prophetic declaration and prayer are a sacred pause, a moment to align your heart with the reality of who you are—a spiritual being hidden with Christ, formed for divine purpose. Let these words wash over you, renewing your mind and positioning you to walk in the freedom of God's perspective.

In the spirit of the Joseph anointing, I declare that I am not defined by the pit of betrayal or the sting of false accusation, but refined by the promise of God's unyielding faithfulness. I choose to live from Heaven's perspective, not Earth's pressure, walking as a spiritual being hidden with Christ in God. My mind is set on things above, my heart governed by the Spirit, and I refuse to bow to fear, delay, or the lies spoken against me. I live above the sun, ruling from the realm I was born of, carrying the favor of a son marked by Heaven.

Father, in the name of Yeshua, I thank You that I am seated with Christ in heavenly places. I repent for every moment I've allowed fear, discouragement, or earthly thinking to cloud my vision. Renew my mind with Your truth and elevate my perspective to see as You see. Teach me to live from my mountain, not merely visit it, training my eyes to discern, my heart to trust, and my words to align with Heaven's blueprint. Today, I choose to set my mind above the sun, dwelling in Your presence and walking in the authority of Your promise. Amen.

Section II – The Breaking

Chapter 4: The Pit and the Process

— Hidden but Not Forgotten —

"They saw him from afar, and before he came near to them they conspired against him to kill him... and they threw him into a pit. The pit was empty; there was no water in it." —Genesis 37:18, 24

The pit is where the dreamer is tested. *The process is where the son is formed.*

You don't truly carry the Joseph Anointing unless you've been thrown into a pit by people who should have loved you. And you don't truly live above the sun until you learn to see purpose in the silence.

I've known the ache of betrayal—not just from strangers, but from those close to me: family, friends, and ministry relationships. I faced seasons of being misjudged and misunderstood, watching trust fracture and my reputation questioned. It felt like a spiritual pit, where everything I'd built seemed to collapse. Yet in that silence, Yahweh met me, whispering purpose into my pain and forming me for His promise. But the pit is not your burial—it is your birth canal. It is the beginning of the process.

The Process Is Holy

We live in a culture that fears pain and fast-tracks promotion. But in the Kingdom, delay is often divine. The anointing must be proven. The word must test you before it can be fulfilled in you (Psalm 105:19).

God doesn't skip steps—He sanctifies them.

"And we know that in all things God works for the good of those who love Him, who have been called according to His purpose." —Romans 8:28

Joseph's pit was his first test: Would he trust the God of the dream when the dream seemed dead? Would he curse the brothers—or cover them with forgiveness in the future?

There are things only the pit can teach you.

In my own journey, I've found that the pit strips what isn't eternal. It removes ego, entitlements, and expectations. It leaves only what Yahweh planted—and it's there, in that stillness, that Holy Spirit begins to whisper destiny again.

Hidden, Not Forgotten

"He made him lord of his house and ruler of all his possessions... until the time that his word came to pass, the word of the Lord tested him."
—Psalm 105:21,19

From the pit to Potiphar's house. From favor to accusation. From responsibility to prison. This is not a linear rise—it's the rollercoaster of refinement.

But none of it is wasted. In *Set Your Mind on Things Above the Sun*, I wrote:

"When you live above the sun, you begin to realize that what looks like delay is actually divine design. You are not being passed over— you are being preserved."

Joseph wasn't punished—*he was hidden*. He was preserved for a moment of national crisis. And you, too, are being preserved. Yahweh never wastes wilderness. What the enemy meant to break you; God is using to build you.

Becoming Before Belonging

We long to be seen. To belong. To be known for what we carry. But in the pit, we learn the gift of becoming before belonging.

Joseph had to become the man who could carry Pharaoh's trust—before Pharaoh ever knew his name. You have to become the person Heaven can trust—*before Earth ever recognizes your mantle.*

In my fourth book: *I Am Mad at Hell—And I'm Not Taking It Anymore!*, I wrote:

"The fire you walk through doesn't destroy you—it brands you. It puts the seal of Heaven on your yes."

You don't come out of the process with titles—**you come out with authority**. And that only comes from pain surrendered, not escaped.

The Anointing That Waits

There's an anointing that comes with action—and there's one that comes with waiting. Joseph's time in prison wasn't just passive suffering. It was prophetic alignment. He was in position when the cupbearer remembered his name.

> *"But when all goes well with you, remember me..."* —Genesis 40:14

This is one of the most vulnerable verses in Joseph's story. It reveals his longing for rescue—and his hope that someone might finally see him. But in asking the cupbearer to intervene, Joseph momentarily placed his hope in man rather than Yahweh.

And the result? Two more years of waiting.

> *"Yet the chief cupbearer did not remember Joseph, but forgot him. When two full years had passed..."* —Genesis 40:23–41:1

This delay wasn't punishment—it was precision. Yahweh wasn't being cruel—He was being exact. Joseph was not forgotten by God... he was being held back for such a time as this.

- There is purpose in the waiting.
- Waiting teaches us to listen again.
- Waiting purifies our motives.
- Waiting positions, us for favor that man could never orchestrate.

I believe some delays we experience are not from the enemy—they are from the Father. They remind us: *"Not by might, nor by power, but by My Spirit,"* says Yahweh of Hosts. —Zechariah 4:6

Personal Reflection – Hidden in the Pit

In that spiritual pit, I felt the weight of betrayal from those I loved—family, friends, ministry relationships. Trust fractured, and my reputation faced shadows I couldn't defend. Yet in that silence, Yahweh met me. He didn't just comfort me—He reshaped me, turning the collapse into a canvas for His promise. A place where no amount of striving could lift me out. A place where only Yahweh's presence could sustain me. I didn't have the answers. I didn't know how long the process would take. But I knew this: God was not finished.

And in the pit, He was purifying me. Not punishing me—forming me. Not destroying me—deepening me.

I remember a season that felt like the deepest pit I'd ever known. Everything that once defined me— my role, my ministry, even my sense of purpose— was stripped away. I found myself sitting alone. Not praying. Not preaching. Not progressing. Just silence. And in that silence, I wasn't sure what was left of me.

But in that silence, something unexpected happened—Yahweh began to speak again. Not about what I had done, but about who I was. He reminded me: the pit wasn't punishment—it was purification. I hadn't been buried. I'd been planted.

I'll never forget the moment I stopped asking Yahweh to lift me out—and started asking Him to take me deeper. That shift didn't erase the pain, but it anchored me in purpose. And in that surrender, the soil of my suffering began to grow something sacred: the first roots of a new season.

Even now, not every relationship has been restored. Some wounds still wait for redemption. But I've seen Yahweh's hand reconcile what once seemed lost forever. I've known the quiet joy of reconnecting with my sons after a season of separation—walking now in healing, honor, and love. That wasn't something I could orchestrate.

That was *The Father's* doing.

So if you find yourself in the pit, take heart. It may feel like a tomb—but it's actually a womb. Something sacred is being formed in you that could never be forged in the palace. Don't rush the process. Don't curse the soil. Yield to the hand of the Potter.

Because *Yahweh wastes nothing. And He always finishes what He starts.*

Here's What I Sense for You Right Now...

Have you been misjudged? Misunderstood? Maybe even by people you trusted the most? I've been there too. It cuts deep. But here's what I've learned: *truth from Holy Spirit always heals deeper than words from people ever could.* Let Him speak into those wounds. Let Him rewrite the narrative others tried to define you by.

And if you're in a season where no one sees you— where doors feel closed and dreams feel distant— don't confuse hiddenness with abandonment. Hidden doesn't mean forgotten; it means preserved. *Yahweh hides what He values.* Ask Him to show you the difference.

Lastly, I want you to honor what the pit has done in you. Yes, it hurt. But it also hollowed out space for holiness. It prepared you. It carved capacity for what's next. *You're not just surviving the pit— you're being sanctified in it.*

You're not who you were. You're becoming someone *Heaven already recognizes.*

So take this to heart:

You are not forgotten—you are hidden for glory. You are not delayed—you are being designed. The pit is not your punishment—it's your preparation. Let the fire refine you. Let the silence shape you. Let the process mature you. Because who you are becoming is already known in Heaven.

And the same God who was with Joseph—is with you. Right now. Right here. In this very moment.

And He's not finished. Not even close.

The Hidden Highway

There was a stretch of my life when I wasn't preaching, teaching, or standing on platforms. I was driving a Motorcoach.

For over three years, I spent more than two-thirds of the year on the road—guiding tour groups through British Columbia, Alberta, as far south as Mount Rushmore, Yellowstone, and the Grand Canyon, and as far north as Alaska and the Yukon.

I'll never forget one journey in particular. I was on the road for 40 days—my wilderness. It began in *late August 2014,* with a *six-day "deadhead"* from *Delta, British Columbia* all the way to *Anchorage, Alaska.* No passengers. Just me, the open road, and Holy Spirit.

But this wasn't just a trip. I was *fleeing Jezebel.*

Not a person—but the spirit behind the chaos I had just escaped. The control, the manipulation, the warfare. I didn't realize it then, but like Elijah in 1 Kings 19, I was running—not in fear, but in *need of healing.* The Lord wasn't punishing me with the wilderness. He was preserving me in it. Like Elijah under the broom tree, I was being fed by the Spirit, carried by grace, and led to a place where the whisper of God could be heard again.

Each day I drove an average of ten hours, winding through rugged mountain passes, valleys, and long stretches of sacred silence. I listened to the Word of God on audio, fed on sermons, and sang until tears soaked the steering wheel. It became a *divine classroom*—and I was being reawakened.

Then something holy began to happen.

Holy Spirit began syncing the worship I played with the scenes I was seeing—the music swelling just as eagles soared overhead, lyrics about God's majesty erupting as snow-capped peaks came into view. Wildlife crossed my path like divine choreography. The road became a sanctuary, the landscape a sermon, and the silence a sacred whisper.

"I was walking through deep personal trauma— not something I had 'gotten over,' but something I was still learning to breathe through. I didn't have a pulpit or a prayer team—but I had Holy Spirit. And He was healing me, mile by mile."

The Word wasn't just information anymore—it was *substance.* Living. Breathing. Active and sharper than any two-edged sword (Hebrews 4:12). It pierced and healed, cut and comforted. Every verse became personal, every promise alive. It washed over me like waves—spirit, soul, and body.

Romans 1:20 came alive: *"For since the creation of the world God's invisible qualities—His eternal power and divine nature—have been clearly seen, being understood from what has been made."*

Creation was testifying.

The *mountains reminded me of Moses,* ascending for revelation. The *stillness echoed Elijah's cave,* where God wasn't in the wind or fire, but in the *gentle whisper* (1 Kings 19:11–13). The vast valleys reminded me that *Joseph had been here too*—not this road, but this process. The hidden years. The misunderstood ones. The anointed yet exiled.

I asked the Lord one day, "Why this route?" And I heard Him whisper, *"Because I'm doing something in the land."*

I asked Him for confirmation.

And then, the *eagles began to appear.*

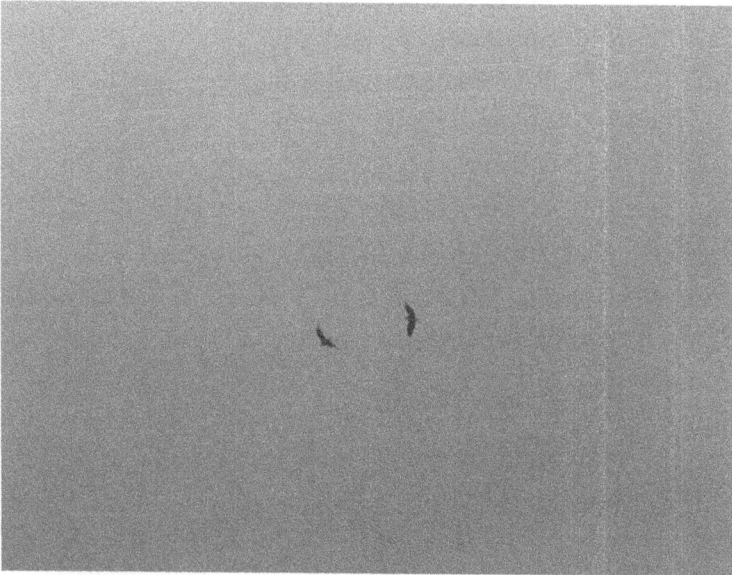

Not once. Not twice. But *again and again*, at nearly every territorial border or prophetic crossing. They met me as I entered cities. They soared above me as I departed. Like divine watchmen, they were signaling what Isaiah had prophesied:

"Those who wait on the Lord shall renew their strength. They shall mount up with wings like eagles..." (Isaiah 40:31).

Eagles have always symbolized the prophetic life. They live in high places. They see what others can't. They soar above the storm rather than flail within it. And they don't flap aimlessly—they glide with precision, catching the wind of Heaven.

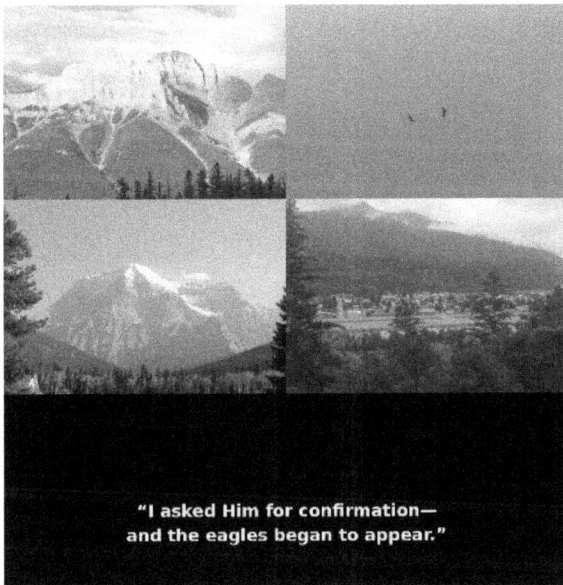

"I asked Him for confirmation— and the eagles began to appear."

Eventually, I picked up the tour group in Anchorage and led them on a *three-week expedition* that felt less like a job and more like a divine assignment. We passed through *Denali, Skagway, Juneau, Whitehorse, Prince Rupert, Jasper, Banff, Wells Gray Provincial Park,* and on to *Whistler, Victoria, and Vancouver.* We experienced the majesty of *Dawson City, Lake Louise, Moraine Lake, Johnston Canyon,* and the grandeur of *Jasper National Park*—then crossed over to *Butchart Gardens* on Vancouver Island.

But I wasn't just leading tourists—I was walking in obedience.

Every stop felt sacred. And at nearly every spiritual crossing, I was met by *eagles in flight*—like messengers from Heaven whispering, *"You're not lost. You're led."*

That season was quiet. Hidden. But deeply holy.

In hotel rooms across Montana, Utah, Arizona, and Nevada—while the world assumed I was "just a driver"—*Yahweh was drawing me closer.* Teaching me to listen again. To trust again. To rest again. I would open my Bible in silence and feel His Presence as strong as any altar I had ever stood behind.

But these weren't just scenic highways. I also faced some of the most *treacherous winter conditions imaginable*—black ice, avalanche zones, whiteouts that swallowed visibility, and stretches of highway where lives had been lost. I've seen trucks spin out in front of me, tires lose grip on sheer ice, and snowstorms so thick I could barely see past the front of the Motorcoach.

And still... I was never alone.

There were moments I shouldn't have made it. But I did.

There were places I shouldn't have had peace.
But I did.

And now, looking back, I understand why.

Yahweh wasn't just preserving my life. He was preparing my spirit.

Those years taught me what no classroom ever could: the pit is not always a place—it's a process.

And sometimes, that process looks like a long highway...

A silent cab...

A snow-covered mountain pass...

A worship song in the dark...

Or an eagle soaring across the sky when you needed it most.

I wasn't being sidelined.

I was being sanctified.

And just like Joseph—I was hidden, but not forgotten.

There are highways no one sees, and wildernesses no one applauds.

But Heaven does.

If you've been walking through your own season of silence...

If the road beneath you feels long, hidden, or misunderstood... This is for you.

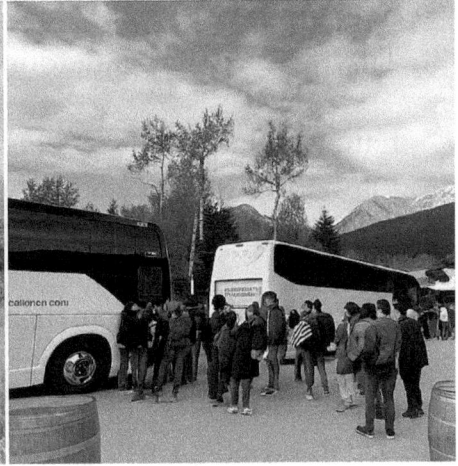

Prophetic Declaration

I declare that my hidden years are not wasted—
they are wombs of purpose.
I am not overlooked. I am being refined in the
fire of God.
Though I walk roads no one celebrates, I walk
them with the favor of Heaven.
I will not confuse hiddenness with
abandonment—*Yahweh hides what He values.*

Even in silence, He is speaking.
Even in pain, He is shaping.
Even in absence, He is present.

This wilderness is not punishment—it is
preparation.
These miles are not meaningless—they are
making me.
This season is not a detour—it is divine design.

I am not fleeing—I am being led.
I am not lost—I am being aligned.
And I am not defeated—I am being delivered.

Like Elijah, I will hear the whisper.
Like Joseph, I will emerge with vision, wisdom,
and authority.
Like the eagle, I will rise—above the storm,
above the noise, above the lies.

I was not cast aside.
I was set apart.

Prayer from the Road

*Father, I thank You for every unseen mile—
every stretch of road You walked with me when
no one else did.
I thank You for the silence that became
sanctuary, and for the wind that reminded me
of Your breath.*

Forgive me for resenting the hiddenness.
Forgive me for believing the lie that I was
forgotten.

Today, I see it clearly: this was holy ground.

I surrender my timeline.
I surrender my need to be understood.
I surrender the ache I carry—the grief that
lingers, the love that feels lost.
You see it all. You feel it with me.
And You walk with me still.

Sanctify this sorrow.
Breathe on this brokenness.
Use even this valley to awaken resurrection life.

Let the eagles remind me of my calling.
Let the mountains remind me of Your covenant.
Let the valleys remind me of Your nearness.
Let the road remind me that I am never alone.

And when the palace doors open,
May I carry the purity, the compassion, and the
authority
That only the wilderness could produce.

I choose to live from above—even when I walk
through the low places.

I choose to listen when no one else sees.
I choose to soar when others settle.

I am Yours.
Use every chapter—every tear, every turn—for
Your glory.

Amen.

Having a Latte in Banff, Alberta

Chapter 5: Legacy of Forgiveness

—Jacob's Grief and Joseph's Redemption

"All his sons and all his daughters came to comfort him, but he refused to be comforted. 'No,' he said, 'I will continue to mourn until I join my son in the grave.'" —Genesis 37:35

The Grief That Lingered

When Joseph's brothers conspired against him, they weren't just hurting their younger sibling— they were setting a fire in their father's heart that would burn for decades. In a single moment of jealousy and betrayal, they robbed Jacob of peace, of closure, of joy. What they meant as a solution to their own insecurity became a generational wound.

Jacob wept, and he kept weeping. The one he loved most was gone, and the sons who remained carried a dark secret. No matter how they tried to comfort him, the Bible says he *refused* to be comforted. He grieved deeply, profoundly—and alone.

This is the cost of betrayal: not only does it crush the victim, but it wounds the innocent. It breaks the hearts of fathers, mothers, children, and spouses. It splits families. It divides homes. And often, those who cause the fracture walk away unaware of the depth of destruction they've unleashed.

Sin Echoes—But So Does Redemption

Family pain rarely stays in one generation. The lies, the deception, the jealousy—it had roots. Remember, Jacob himself once deceived his father, Isaac. The cloak of goatskin that covered his arms would eventually mirror the bloodstained cloak of Joseph. What was hidden in one generation echoed in the next.

But here's the good news: *the pattern didn't end in betrayal*—it ended in forgiveness.

Joseph had every right to retaliate. He held all the power, all the authority. But when the time came, he chose mercy over revenge. He didn't just feed his brothers—he embraced them. He didn't expose them—he wept with them. And in doing so, Joseph broke a generational cycle.

"You intended to harm me, but God intended it for good... to save many lives." (Genesis 50:20)

Wounded to Be Used - *Forgiveness is the Legacy*

We break generational bondage *not* by repeating the pain, but by choosing a better path.

Forgiveness is not weakness—it's warfare. It dismantles the enemy's strategy of division. It heals wounds that bitterness only makes deeper. It silences the voice of revenge and makes way for legacy.

Joseph's dreams did come true. He did rise. He did rule. But the true beauty of the story isn't just in his elevation—it's in the *restoration*.

- His brothers were redeemed.
- His father's heart was healed.
- A family was reunited.
- And a people group—an entire future—was preserved.

This is what happens when forgiveness reigns.

Your Family is Worth Fighting For

You may be standing in the middle of a divided house right now.

Maybe betrayal, misunderstanding, or silence has separated you from those you love. Maybe like Jacob, you've mourned in isolation, wondering if healing will ever come.

A Father's Heart Still Hopes

My heart has always been for my family—my children, my grandchildren, those I hold closest. There have been seasons where I longed for deeper connection, for shared moments of joy, faith, and togetherness.

Yet, life's complexities sometimes created distance, not by choice, but through the unfolding of time and circumstance.

The absence wasn't a refusal of love—it was a space where God was quietly working.

In those moments, I turned to prayer, lifting my loved ones before Yahweh, asking Him to draw them near, to guide their paths, and to weave our stories together in His perfect timing.

One morning, as I prayed for their peace and joy, I sensed Holy Spirit's gentle whisper: *"Love them where they are."* I began writing blessings over them—for their dreams, their journeys, their hearts to know God's love.

Those prayers didn't erase the longing, but they anchored me in hope, filling me with expectancy for what God is doing.

Like Jacob, I carry a father's heart that hopes and trusts in God's redemptive plan. I've learned that love doesn't demand immediate answers—it sows seeds of grace, trusting the harvest to God.

My prayers for my family are alive, and I believe He is moving in ways I may not yet see.

I know the quiet ache of longing for those I love. It's not a pain that shouts, but one that lingers softly, waiting for God's touch.

There are family members I've dreamed of walking closer with, sharing laughter, faith, and legacy.

Those moments haven't fully come, but I hold them in my heart, trusting God's timing. In the stillness, I've found Him faithful—present in every prayer, every hope, every tear.

One morning, as I carried this longing, I chose to release the weight of waiting and embrace God's invitation to bless.

I prayed for my children and grandchildren, asking for His peace, His presence, and His joy to surround them.

It wasn't about fixing the distance—it was about aligning my heart with Heaven's love.

That choice brought freedom, not because every question was answered, but because I trusted God to write the next chapter.

If restoration comes—slowly, gently, in God's way—I'll meet it with open arms and a heart full of joy.

Forgiveness, for me, isn't about rewriting the past; it's about making room for a future where love prevails.

It's a choice to trust Yahweh's heart for my family, knowing He's weaving a story of healing.

So don't give up. Don't let the silence deceive you. Yahweh is not finished writing your story.

The same God who reunited Joseph and Jacob is still at work—moving hearts, aligning moments, and redeeming what you thought was lost forever.

Let Joseph be your model: choose forgiveness, speak mercy, and build bridges. Your legacy won't be marked by the pain you endured, but by the healing you released.

Allow me to speak prophetically into your heart— the place bearing the weight of hidden wounds, family brokenness, or inherited pain.

You may carry the scars of betrayal in your body, choices, or silence, but as a son or daughter of God (Galatians 3:26-28, NLT), you are not defined by that pain, you are called to rise.

Like Joseph, you are called to rise above it, letting Yahweh's healing transform your scars into a testimony of purpose.

But you are not powerless. You are not bound to repeat what broke those before you. You are not stuck in the cycle—you are standing at the threshold of redemption.

Maybe you've carried Jacob's grief—the quiet mourning of what was lost long ago.

Maybe no one ever taught you how to forgive what still hurts.

But Holy Spirit is here—not to erase your pain, but to walk you through it.

To touch what others overlooked. To heal what betrayal fractured.

And if no one has ever told you this before, hear it now—clear and prophetic:

In your generation, the curse stops.

In your family, forgiveness reigns.

Your legacy is mercy, and your future is free.

So let these words rise within you—not just as encouragement, but as a commissioning:

Prophetic Declaration

I am not the product of division—I am the vessel of restoration.

I do not carry bitterness—I carry blessing.

What the enemy fractured, Yahweh is healing.

I will not repeat generational sin—I will redeem it through obedience and love.

I am not bound by what was—I am anchored in what's to come.

Like Joseph, I've been positioned to restore what others abandoned.

My story will not end in silence—it will echo with mercy.

And the God of Jacob will turn my mourning into joy. Amen.

Reflection

What scars is Yahweh calling you to transform into a testimony of purpose?

But even in the ache of what was lost, Yahweh was writing a redemptive future through my lineage— just like Joseph's sons would one day testify.

Chapter 6: Forgiveness and the Family Line

— *Healing What Tried to Destroy You* —

"But Joseph said to them, 'Do not fear, for am I in the place of God? As for you, you meant evil against me, but God meant it for good...' Genesis 50:19–20

Forgiveness is not forgetting. It is not denial. It is Kingdom justice—releasing what tried to destroy you so Heaven can redeem it.

The most profound act of authority in Joseph's life was not when he interpreted Pharaoh's dream or when he governed Egypt—it was when he wept on the shoulders of his brothers. The ones who threw him into the pit. The ones who stripped his robe, silenced his voice, and sold his future.

And he forgave them.

He fed the ones who betrayed him. He protected the ones who plotted his ruin. He wept over the ones who never came looking for him.

That's reformation. That's family healing. That's the heart of the Father manifest in a son.

The Wound and the Wisdom

"Joseph could no longer control himself before all his attendants, and he cried out... Then he wept so loudly that the Egyptians heard him." — Genesis 45:1–2

The pain ran deep. But Joseph did not bury it—he processed it. He let it break open before it broke him down. His weeping wasn't weakness—it was holy release. Forgiveness didn't erase his memory—***it redeemed it***.

When you live *above the sun*, you see that the people who hurt you are not your real enemy. The real enemy is the cycle. The pattern. The spiritual inheritance of betrayal, fear, pride, silence, favoritism, abandonment.

Joseph didn't just forgive his brothers—*he cut off the power of generational cycles.*

In my experience, *"God doesn't just deliver you from your enemies—He delivers you from becoming like them."*

You Cannot Heal What You Will Not Face

Healing the family line means walking straight into what wounded you. It means naming the pain, dismantling the lie, and refusing to carry forward what Yahweh never authored.

"He has sent Me to heal the brokenhearted, to proclaim liberty to the captives, and the opening of the prison to those who are bound..." —Isaiah 61:1

When Joseph stood before his brothers, he saw the *Divine Purpose*, not just the human pain.

"It was not you who sent me here, but God..." — Genesis 45:8

This is not blindness. *This is spiritual sight.* Joseph reframed betrayal as divine strategy. *He elevated truth over trauma.*

You cannot change your history—*but in Christ, you can redeem your heritage.*

Forgiveness Is the Key to Legacy

Joseph's legacy wasn't his title—it was the fact that he preserved a family. A family through which Messiah would one day come.

What if your healing is the gatekeeper to your children's inheritance? What if your forgiveness unlocks a future you'll never see—but your descendants will walk in?

In *Set Your Mind on Things Above the Sun*, I wrote:

"Legacy is not built by holding on—it's built by letting go. Some of the greatest breakthroughs will be seen not in our lifetime, but in the fruit of our surrender."

A New Line Starts with You

Joseph's words echo through the generations:

"You meant evil against me, but God meant it for good..." —Genesis 50:20 *That is the cry of a generational reformer.*

That is the mantle of a Joseph.

You are not here to repeat the curse—*you are here to redeem the bloodline.* You are not here to survive—*you are here to build an altar of forgiveness in the place where pain once ruled.*

The Joseph Anointing is not just about governing nations—***it's about healing homes***.

You may not have chosen the dysfunction—but by the Spirit of Yahweh, you can choose to end it.

Personal Reflection – Loving Through the Distance, Forgiving into the Future

My heart carries a deep love for my family—my children, my grandchildren, and those Yahweh has woven into my life's scroll. There have been seasons where I longed for closer connection, for shared moments of faith, joy, and unity. Life's unfolding often brought distance—not from malice, but from mystery. I used to ache over what was missing, but in those quiet places, I met God in a deeper way. His presence was not absent in the silence; it was forming something sacred.

There were days I didn't understand the distance—only felt its ache. Moments when I was seen in ways I couldn't explain or control. But over time, I stopped asking, *"Why did this happen?"* and began asking, *"What does Heaven want to redeem through this?"* That question changed everything.

Holy Spirit whispered to my heart one day, *"Love them where they are."* That invitation became my rhythm. I began writing blessings over my children and grandchildren—not to fix what felt distant, but to align my heart with Heaven's vision. I prayed not just for healing, but for destiny. Not just for reconciliation, but for revelation. My love didn't shrink—it expanded.

And then came another whisper—this time, through the prayer of Stephen: *"Lord, do not hold this sin against them."* That prayer pierced something deep in me. Forgiveness, I realized, wasn't only about letting go of what had happened—it was about making room for what God still desired to do. It wasn't about pretending it didn't hurt. It was about refusing to let the pain keep writing the story.

In that space, I discovered what real forgiveness is: it's loving through the ache, praying through the silence, and trusting Yahweh's redemptive timeline. Like Joseph in Egypt, I learned that vindication is not the highest aim—restoration is. What others may have meant for harm, God is already turning for good. That truth anchored me.

I remember standing in my grandson's room one night, watching him sleep—peaceful, unburdened. And the Lord whispered, *"This is what redemption looks like."* In that moment, I saw more than a child—I saw a generation healed. I saw laughter where silence used to reign. Connection where rejection once ruled.

Something shifted that night. Not just in me, but in the atmosphere of my family line.

Forgiveness isn't weakness—it's a weapon. It breaks generational cycles. It silences the spirit of accusation. It removes the grip of offense and plants a seed of legacy. You're not just forgiving the past—you're planting hope for the future. You're not just breaking a curse—you're birthing a new storyline.

I didn't grow up with a roadmap for this kind of healing. I had to walk it out through surrender, through scars, through the sacred silence of mercy. But I can tell you now: the curse has broken. The blessing has begun.

If pain has tried to define your identity—if silence has tried to bury your story—let Yahweh speak louder. You are not what was done to you. You are not what was lost. You are His. Chosen. Healed. Commissioned. This... is the shift. This... is the start.

So, whether or not every relationship has come full circle—my heart is at peace. My spirit is unburdened. My love remains open. This is the legacy I carry now. Not one of distance, but of expectation. Not of pain, but of promise.

The Blessing that Reverses the Curse:

Ephraim and Manasseh — Redeeming the Line

Joseph didn't just forgive his past—*he reshaped the future through his sons.*

When he named them, he was *prophesying healing into his bloodline.*

"Joseph named the firstborn Manasseh, saying, 'God has made me forget all my trouble and all my father's household.' He named the second Ephraim, saying, 'God has made me fruitful in the land of my suffering.'" —Genesis 41:51–52

Manasseh means *"causing to forget."*

Ephraim means *"double fruitfulness."*

It's no coincidence that fruitfulness followed forgiveness.

Joseph refused to name his sons after pain—*he named them after promise.* He would not let the betrayal of brothers become the banner over his children. His family's future wouldn't be shaped by bitterness—it would be marked by blessing.

And then came the moment of generational transfer.

In Genesis 48, when Jacob went to bless Joseph's sons, *he crossed his hands.* He placed his right hand—*the hand of covenant blessing*—on Ephraim, the younger, instead of Manasseh, the firstborn. Joseph tried to correct him, but Jacob said, *"I know, my son, I know..."* and blessed them both.

That crossing of hands wasn't random. It was prophetic reversal. It was Yahweh saying, *"I am not limited by your birth order, your brokenness, or your past. I am the God who redeems it all."*

The cycle of pain was breaking. The old patterns of favoritism, jealousy, and striving were coming to an end.

Joseph had broken the curse—and Jacob, the father who once favored sons to the harm of others, was now participating in redemption.

That's the power of forgiveness. It doesn't just set you free—it heals backwards and blesses forward.

It redeems the generations.

And so once again, we echo Joseph's words:

"You meant it for evil. But God meant it for good. To save many lives."

I choose forgiveness—not because they deserve it, but because I am free.

I choose to bless, not just survive. To restore, not just recover. To rewrite the future by releasing the past.

I declare over my life and yours:

I choose forgiveness—not because they deserve it, but because I am free.

I break every generational curse and cancel every soul tie to trauma.

I reclaim my family line for Yahweh.

I walk in the wisdom of Joseph and the mercy of Christ.

I sow peace into the places I was wounded.

I will not reproduce what I was delivered from.

The healing begins with me.

And the legacy starts now.

Let this not just be the conclusion of a chapter—but the commissioning of a new season.

Let this be your prayer:

Father, I thank You for the blood of Yeshua that speaks a better word over my family line.

Today, I release those who hurt me. I forgive those who misunderstood me. I bless those who betrayed me.

Yahweh, I ask You to break every cycle of pain, pride, silence, addiction, abandonment, or fear.

Heal the places I cannot see. Cleanse the history I did not choose.

I declare: it ends with me—and it begins with You.

Let my life be an altar of redemption.

Let my legacy be soaked in Your mercy.

Use me, like Joseph, to feed the very ones who once rejected me.

In the name of Yeshua, Amen.

This is not the end —it is the beginning of generational healing.

Because what the enemy meant for evil... *Yahweh is still turning for good.*

To save many lives—and to set the generations free.

Yet while blessings were being born, betrayal still echoed behind me—and the pit of rejection hadn't yet lost its sting...

Chapter 7: Cancelled But Not Conquered

The Sting of Prophetic Betrayal

There is nothing new under the sun. Joseph's betrayal wasn't merely personal—it was prophetic. His brothers didn't just resent his dreams; they were enraged by the weight of his calling. The dreamer awakened their insecurities, so they conspired to cancel him—stripping his coat, casting him into a pit, and selling him into slavery. Then they masked their actions in goat's blood and deception (Genesis 37:19–20, 31–32). It wasn't enemies who betrayed him—it was family, the ones who knew him best.

Betrayal rarely comes from enemies. More often, it comes from those closest to us—those we once trusted with our hearts and our history. That's what made Joseph's betrayal so devastating. It wasn't just personal; it was prophetic. His brothers didn't merely dislike him—they were disturbed by his dreams. The favor on his life exposed the fear in theirs. The dreamer awakened something they weren't ready to confront.

So they stripped his coat, tossed him into a pit, and sold him into silence. Then they masked their betrayal in blood, crafting a story that covered shame with deception.

That spirit still lives today—jealousy dressed in loyalty, fear dressed in concern, deception cloaked in half-truths. Sometimes it comes not through a violent act, but through a whisper. A social post. A group text.

A trusted voice reshaping a chapter of your life you've long surrendered to God. And the blow doesn't always stop with you—it can ripple into generations. Innocent ones carry the silence. Your name is reshaped in rooms you'll never walk into. Legacies, momentarily shadowed, wait for the light to break through.

I've felt that sting. I've known what it is to be misunderstood, to have a chapter re-read through a bitter lens rather than the blood of Yeshua.

But I've also come to see what Joseph saw: **what was meant for evil, God uses for good.** The pit is not your end. It's the place where purpose is purified.

In one of my hardest seasons, when connection with family felt fractured and unfixable, I heard Holy Spirit whisper, *"Will you love them anyway?"* That question didn't erase the ache—it transformed it. I began to bless my children and grandchildren. Not with demands, but with declarations. Not with pressure, but with prayer. I asked Yahweh to walk with them, to guide them, to write their stories with grace. Those prayers became my bridge. Love replaced longing. Hope replaced heaviness.

Joseph didn't just survive betrayal—he was shaped by it. Refined. Prepared. Positioned. The betrayal became his bootcamp. And the same is true for you.

You may have been misjudged. Silenced. Rewritten. But your identity is not in what they said. It's in what God spoke.

Betrayal does not void your destiny.

In fact, it may just be the very soil where your calling takes root.

So if you're walking through a season of betrayal—especially from those you once held close—remember: Joseph's story didn't end in the pit. It didn't end in prison. It ended in purpose. And yours will, too.

The Pit as Divine Preparation

Joseph's pit wasn't his grave—it was his gateway.

The prison didn't silence his gift—it refined it. In confinement, his character was forged, his discernment sharpened, and his compassion deepened.

Even while bleeding, Joseph served others— interpreting dreams not his own, while waiting for the fulfillment of his own (Genesis 39:20–23).

The prison wasn't a dead end; it was a training ground. Before he preserved nations, he ministered in chains.

I've walked through those spiritual prisons— seasons of injustice, loss, and isolation where everything I thought was secure was stripped away.

Relationships I believed were unshakable collapsed. Positions I once held with confidence were removed.

The future I envisioned dissolved into silence and uncertainty. I cried out in the stillness, *"Why this path? Why this pain?"* No thunder answered— but a knowing settled in: *this was not punishment. It was preparation.*

In that wilderness, Holy Spirit whispered in ways I had never heard before. With the applause gone and titles stripped away, I discovered the only identity that endures—beloved son. The breaking didn't diminish me—it revealed me. It carved authority, refined empathy, and birthed a voice forged in fire. What once looked like abandonment became the place of encounter.

Looking back, I see it now—every closed door, every misunderstood moment, was God's hand refining me. As Psalm 105:17–22 says, Joseph *"was sold as a slave... until the time came to fulfill his dreams."* That time came—and so will yours. The deeper the wound, the deeper the well God draws from when He chooses to pour out His glory.

Your pain is not wasted. It's forging something eternal.

Joseph's Redemptive Restraint: The Power You Don't Use

When Joseph stood before his brothers in Egypt— face to face with the very ones who betrayed him— he held the power to expose their sin, humiliate their guilt, and pronounce judgment. He had the evidence. He had the right. And yet... he cleared the room.

"Then Joseph could no longer control himself before all his attendants, and he cried out, 'Have everyone leave my presence!'" (Genesis 45:1).

 What followed wasn't public justice—it was private mercy. Joseph didn't just forgive them— he covered them. He didn't retell the story of their hatred, the pit, or the lie they spun with goat's blood. He protected Benjamin, who had lived for years beneath the weight of their deception. He shielded their shame instead of spotlighting it.

This is the mark of mature authority: mercy when vengeance is justified. Restraint when retaliation would feel righteous. Vindication may feed the ego—but legacy requires surrender.

I remember that crossroad.

There was a moment when my past—long healed and covered by the blood of Yeshua—was weaponized, not by enemies, but by those I had shared life with. It wasn't about justice; it was about framing a false narrative rooted in old bitterness. The blow cut deep—not just the lie itself, but the silence of those who knew the truth and said nothing. That silence rang louder than accusation. I grieved. I prayed. I wept.

And then I heard Holy Spirit ask:

"Will you let Me be your Defender? Will you protect what I've already redeemed?"

Everything in me wanted to speak out—to correct the record, to clear my name. But I heard another whisper, a deeper call: *legacy over litigation.* That's when I laid it down. I chose mercy, not because I had no voice—but because I had been refined by the fire. I blessed those who cursed me. I covered what could have been exposed.

Some relationships never came back. But I didn't lose—I was freed.

This is the mantle of the Joseph anointing. Not just to interpret dreams, but to protect futures. Not just to endure betrayal, but to respond with restraint.

Anyone can expose a wound—only the healed can guard a legacy.

My heart is clean. My hands are open. And my spirit is free.

That's the testimony I carry—not because I won the argument, but because I surrendered to the greater assignment.

Living Above the Sun

To live above the sun is to live beyond offense. It's choosing grace when you've been misjudged, mercy when you've been mistreated, and surrender when everything in you wants to fight back. This is where the Joseph anointing matures—from revelation to authority, from calling to character.

Joseph didn't just survive betrayal—*he transcended it.*

He walked in *purity* when falsely accused.

He served in *integrity* when unjustly forgotten.

He responded with *mercy* when face-to-face with his betrayers.

He didn't let the voices of brothers, the systems of Egypt, or the weight of injustice define him. His heart was anchored in a higher reality.

That's what it means to *live above the sun*—to see your story through the eyes of eternity.

Cancel culture may echo loudly in the courts of man, but heaven holds the final verdict.

"You meant it for evil," Joseph told his brothers, "but God meant it for good, to bring about that many people should be kept alive" (Genesis 50:20).

Your destiny isn't shaped by viral posts, whispered slander, or family betrayals. It's held— securely— in the hands of a sovereign Father. What God ordains, He sustains. What He anoints, He appoints. And what He allows, He uses for His glory.

That truth rewrote my story.

In the wilderness, as the fire refined me, I made a declaration over my bloodline:

The curse of exposure ends here.

The spirit of Jezebel will not write our story—
mercy will.

Restoration will not skip a generation—it will find my children's children.

Where pain once ruled, I built an altar of forgiveness and laid every offense down.

I chose to live untethered from bitterness.

Rooted in heaven.

Hidden in Christ.

Anchored above the sun.

A Wilderness That Shapes You

The wilderness is not punishment—it's preparation.

It's not rejection—it's refinement.

It's not the end—it's the proving ground between promise and promotion.

Joseph didn't ascend to the palace overnight. Between the robe and the throne came a wilderness marked by betrayal, accusation, silence, and confinement. But none of it was wasted. The pit was a setup. The prison was a school. The silence was sacred. And the suffering? It was part of the sanctifying fire.

In that hidden place, Joseph learned to *serve while bleeding*, to *prophesy while waiting*, and to *trust while forgotten* (Genesis 40:5–23). His gifts weren't discovered in the palace—they were sharpened in the shadows. Every delay refined his discernment. Every injustice forged his humility.

Every forgotten promise carved deeper dependency on God.

I know that road well.

I didn't ask for it. But I wouldn't trade what it forged in me.

My mantle wasn't birthed behind microphones.

It was formed in midnight prayers, forged in misunderstood seasons, and tempered in the fire of rejection. I had walked the road of repentance long before the accusation resurfaced—held accountable by spiritual fathers, restored by the grace of Yeshua, and rebuilt through time, tears, and truth.

But when the lie came back—repackaged for harm, not healing—I faced the wilderness all over again.

In that wilderness, I was stripped of every platform and title I once leaned on. I wanted to speak up, to clarify, to defend. But instead, God drew me deeper. And in the absence of applause, I rediscovered my truest identity: **beloved son**.

In the ashes of disappointment, I saw the silhouette of a new mantle—one not shaped by striving but surrendered through fire. My voice didn't rise from vindication; it rose from the refining. My authority didn't come from position; it came from the wilderness.

As Romans 8:28 declares, *"All things work together for good to those who love God, to those who are called according to His purpose."* Not just the obvious victories—but the betrayals, the tears, the slander, and the silence. In God's hands, **nothing is wasted**.

Encouragement for the Wounded

If you're reading this with a broken heart—betrayed, misjudged, or quietly grieving what was taken—I see you.

More importantly, God sees you. He's not absent in the pit. He's not silent in the prison.

He's right there, forging something eternal in the unseen.

Let me remind you:

You are not being *buried*—you are being *planted*.

The pit hasn't canceled your calling—*it's refining it*.

Your name may have been dragged through the mud, but your identity is still anchored in heaven.

You are not disqualified. You are being *qualified* by fire.

Let Holy Spirit Walk you back through every wound—not to relive it, but to redeem it.

Let Him anoint the parts of your story that still feel raw. Let Him speak into the silence.

The oil that flows from your life won't come from comfort—it will come from the crushing.

And the anointing you carry will not be borrowed from another man's fire.

It will be your own, lit in the wilderness, tended in the dark, and revealed in due time.

Your voice will carry weight not because you escaped the pain—but because you met God in it.

The fire didn't consume you—it commissioned you.

The betrayal didn't end your story —it authenticated it.

So let this truth rise—not just as encouragement, but as a prophetic decree over your life:

Refining is not rejection. Breaking is not the end. Your wilderness is not a waste.

God is not punishing you—He's preparing you.

Every unseen prayer, every night of weeping, every slanderous whisper—it's all being woven into a testimony that will set others free.

You're not being disqualified—you're being distilled. Your mantle is maturing. Your authority is deepening.

And you, beloved... are not forgotten.

Prophetic Declaration

I am not cancelled —I am called.

I am not erased —I am established.

I am not rejected—I am restored.

I rise above lies, betrayal, and silence —anointed for legacy, hidden in Christ.

Every season of breaking is birthing something sacred.

Where there was loss, God releases blessing.

Where there was abandonment, He draws near.

What the enemy meant for evil, my Father is using for good.

My life will testify:

"He brought me out to bring me in." (Psalm 40:2)

Selah: Forged in Fire

"It is doubtful whether God can bless a man greatly until He has hurt him deeply." — A.W. Tozer

Joseph's journey—from pit to prison to palace—reveals a sacred pattern: *favor often follows fire.*

Before the crown came betrayal. Before influence came false accusation. Before elevation came abandonment.

And yet—God used every wound as preparation, not punishment.

Psalm 105:17–22 declares that God *"sent a man before them—Joseph—sold as a slave... until the time came to fulfill his dreams."*

The pit, the prison, and the pain were not detours—they were divine design.

This same pattern is echoed in Scripture again and again:

David was hunted before he was crowned.

Moses was exiled before he was commissioned.

Jesus was crushed in Gethsemane before He rose in glory.

And now—you.

Your wilderness is not your end.

Your pain is not wasted.

The breaking is not your defeat—it's the forging of your destiny.

So trust the fire. Trust the silence. Trust the long road.

The deeper the wound, the deeper the well He draws from.

This chapter may feel buried in shadows, but resurrection always follows the cross.

From the ashes of betrayal, God is calling you to rise:

Not as a victim—but as a vessel.

Not as one cancelled—but as one crowned.

To reign with wisdom, walk in purity, and **build for reformation**—a theme we now enter in Section III.

 Note: For deeper insight into Joseph's mercy, the pain of exposure, and the breaking of generational curses through forgiveness, see the Addendum titled:

"Reflections from the Pit: Deeper Insights on Betrayal and Redemption."

It was in the quiet crucible of being cancelled that I discovered what could never be taken: sonship, identity, and the grace to build again.

Section III – The Rising
Chapter 8: Reigning with Wisdom

Prophet: Speaking with Discernment and Authority

Joseph's transition from prisoner to prime minister didn't begin with a promotion—it began with a prophetic word.

When he stood before Pharaoh, Joseph didn't just interpret a dream. He released Heaven's strategy. He didn't perform—he operated. He didn't posture—he flowed in divine authority. He operated as a prophet—one who could see, discern, and build.

This is a crucial pillar of the Joseph Anointing: the prophetic mantle that carries divine discernment. It's not merely about visions or dreams—it's about spiritual architecture. Prophets in this hour must not only declare what's coming; they must prepare the people to walk through it.

I've lived this in my own journey. There were moments when Yahweh gave me a word that shifted the direction of a situation, a ministry, or even a life. These weren't casual insights—they were Heaven's blueprints. And I've learned that the authority to speak doesn't come from eloquence—it comes from intimacy. From listening long enough to echo the voice of the Lord.

Joseph was not performing before Pharaoh. He was functioning in his anointing. This is what prophets do: they interpret the unseen and align the present with the future God intends.

— Building What Heaven Designed —

"Then Pharaoh said to Joseph, 'Since God has made all this known to you, there is no one so discerning and wise as you. You shall be in charge of my palace... Only with respect to the throne will I be greater than you.'" — Genesis 41:39–40

- *Joseph didn't strive for a throne—he was summoned to one.*
- *He didn't chase influence —influence chased him. And when it came, he was ready.*

This is the essence of *the Joseph Anointing*: you are not crowned by the world—*you are commissioned by Heaven.*

The same man who once wept in a pit is now interpreting the dreams of kings. The same boy whose voice was silenced is now setting the course of nations. This is not a fairytale—it's the divine pattern for every son and daughter willing to embrace the process.

Learning to Reign with Wisdom

Wisdom doesn't always shout. Sometimes, she whispers through creation.

In Matthew 6, Yeshua reminds us to *"look at the birds."* For me, that's become more than a metaphor—it's a divine rhythm.

I see eagles often, and almost always in moments where Yahweh is inviting me into deeper wisdom.

They appear when I'm wrestling with decisions, preparing for transition, or seeking clarity from above.

These sightings aren't random—they're reminders.

Wisdom shows me the patterns of Heaven, not just the problems on earth. And over time, I've learned that promotion doesn't begin with the throne—it begins with the perspective. Joseph didn't rise because he was the loudest voice in the room. He rose because he carried Heaven's solution in an earthly crisis.

I've experienced that firsthand. Just before seasons of breakthrough, I often feel the weight of the pit—the delay, the silence, the pressing. But that's when Wisdom draws near. That's when Holy Spirit begins to reveal Yahweh's blueprint, just as Jeremiah 29:11 declares: *"For I know the plans I have for you, declares the Lord..."*

My part is not to create the path. My part is to walk in the steps He's already ordered.

Reigning with wisdom isn't about controlling the outcome—it's about partnering with Heaven, trusting that even when I can't see the palace, I can still soar like the eagle.

The Wisdom to Reign

"Since God has made all this known to you..."
Genesis 41:39

Joseph's authority didn't come from politics or personality—it came from revelation.

Pharaoh didn't promote Joseph because of ambition. He saw the wisdom of Yahweh on him.

Wisdom is the proof of maturity. Not just dreams—but interpretation. Not just vision—but administration.

You can have a prophetic gift and still lack the wisdom to govern.

Joseph's anointing was not just to dream—*it was to build what Heaven revealed.*

In *Set Your Mind on Things Above the Sun*, I wrote: *"When you think from Heaven's seat, you begin to rule from Heaven's plan."*

Kingdom Blueprints Require Kingdom Mindsets

Joseph did not impose Egyptian solutions. *He brought Heaven's strategy.*

His idea to create storehouses in the years of plenty was not just economic policy—*it was prophetic stewardship.*

He didn't just save Egypt—he preserved the family of Jacob, *the bloodline of covenant.*

When you rule with wisdom, you build for both the now and the not-yet. You create systems that sustain nations—and legacies.

Joseph didn't just interpret seasons—he prepared for them. He didn't just react—he responded with strategy born in the Spirit.

This is the kind of wisdom Yahweh is awakening in this generation: prophetic, practical, Spirit-led reformers who know how to govern with insight and build what Heaven reveals.

The Anointing to Solve Problems

"Can we find anyone like this man, one in whom is the spirit of God?" —Genesis 41:38

When Heaven's wisdom rests on you, you become the solution no one saw coming.

You may not have a title, but the presence on your life will be undeniable. Joseph never had to promote himself—Pharaoh did it for him.

You were not called just to point out problems—you were called to carry Kingdom solutions. This world is aching for leaders like Joseph:

- Dreamers who don't drift
- Builders who don't boast

- Sons who serve with royalty in their bones

Sons Who Build

Joseph didn't rule like Pharaoh—*he ruled like a son.* He used his power to provide, not to punish.

He didn't exact revenge—*he distributed provision.* And through it all, he never forgot who he was.

Even in Egypt, he never stopped being Hebrew. In other words, *even surr*

ounded by influence, he never lost his integrity. Even in royalty, *he never stopped being a son.*

That is wisdom. That is identity. That is Kingdom.

Forged in the Flames

A season came when the progress I'd built over years ground to a halt—not for lack of vision, but because Yahweh was drawing me deeper. Having walked through seasons of loss, public misunderstanding, and deep surrender, I found myself invited again to trust Yahweh with what I once thought was permanent. Yet, the calling still burned within me. The anointing still rested on me. The dream still blazed in my heart. But I was weary—not of the ministry, but of the noise surrounding it.

In a quiet moment of surrender, Holy Spirit pierced me with a question deeper than any strategy or leadership meeting could reach: *"Will you build out of fear... or from the fire?"* That question unraveled me. Would I build to prove myself... or to stay faithful to the dream Yahweh whispered in the dark? Or would I build from what was forged in the pit, refined in the prison, and whispered in the wilderness? God wasn't asking for performance— He sought purity. Not results—He sought surrender.

That day, I returned to the divine blueprints— quiet instructions birthed in the dark, carrying eternal weight in my spirit. I laid aside voices demanding what *should* be done and leaned into the One who had always led me faithfully: the voice of the Lord. Like Joseph, I chose to carry a pattern, not a platform—a divine strategy born from stillness, not striving; from private encounters, not public approval.

Joseph's wisdom was forged in the fire of adversity. He didn't build to impress Pharaoh or prove his brothers wrong. He built storehouses to carry God's heart, saving nations in famine (Genesis 41:46–49). That's how I choose to build now—not to recover lost years or gain applause, but to obey. And I've learned this truth: *when you build as a son, Yahweh backs it.* He sends provision, aligns people, and breathes life into the work. He's not building monuments to ego—*He's building vessels for His glory.*

Let me speak to you now. You didn't endure the fire just to survive it—you emerged with wisdom; *a mantle forged in the flames.* You may not have stood before Pharaoh, but you've stood through storms. You've wept in hidden places, been refined in silence. Through it all, God shaped something in you that can't be taught—only lived.

So, pause and write down what the fire taught you. Own it. That's part of your anointing. Then ask: *Am I building what God dreamed for me, or what others expect?* This is your moment to lead— not from striving, but from sonship; not to impress, but to reform. What's forged in the fire will stand in the famine, carrying His Presence for a legacy that outlives you (Psalm 105:17–22).

A Son Who Builds

My heart has never chased platforms or applause—that was never the dream. From the beginning, I longed for Yahweh's Presence, to walk with Him in quiet places, to hear His voice not to impress, but to obey. Through every delay, betrayal, and unopened door, I learned a truth more valuable than fame: *how to build with Heaven.* The Joseph anointing isn't forged by striving—it's shaped in silence, refined in hidden places, and tested by fire (Psalm 105:17–22). It doesn't demand attention; it stands ready when the time comes.

Like Joseph, I no longer just dream—I prepare. I carry wisdom forged in trials, rising with strategy and grace. I don't need to be seen—I need to be faithful. I refuse to lead like a servant begging for notice. I lead as a son, secure in who I belong to, building not to echo man's systems but to fulfill Heaven's design. My posture is clear: *to build what I see in the Spirit, to store what others will need, to reform what's broken—not to impress, but to obey.* The Joseph anointing rests on me, calling me to lead in love, build in wisdom, and carry a legacy that outlives me.

'He who has an ear, let him hear what the Spirit is saying' (Revelation 2:7): The fire you've walked through has forged you to stand in God's purpose, not to chase man's approval. You carry a mantle refined by trials; a wisdom shaped in silence. Like Joseph, you were born to build storehouses for *Yahweh's glory*, not platforms for praise. Ask yourself: *Am I stewarding Heaven's call?* As a *son or daughter of God* (Galatians 3:26-28), embrace *the Joseph anointing*—lead to serve, build what endures, and *trust Yahweh* to *breathe life* into your obedience.

Commissioning Prayer

Abba Father, Yahweh,

You have shaped me in hidden places, teaching me more in stillness than in the spotlight. Every trial, including the prison of pain, has deepened my capacity for Your Presence.

Every tear has sown wisdom. Every test has refined my trust in You. I receive the Joseph anointing—the grace to hear, see, and build above the sun according to Your design, not for my name, but for Your glory.

Guide my hands to steward my family, impact my generation, and sow for those yet to come. Give me wisdom to build storehouses that nourish in famine, precision to walk in Your blueprints, and peace to lead in step with Your Spirit. I don't seek a throne—I seek Your whisper. I don't desire to rule—I desire to reign with You.

Make me a faithful builder, a vessel of Your heart, creating what testifies of You and endures beyond me. As Your son, I rise in humility, obedience, and the name of Yeshua.

Amen.

Chapter 9: The Storehouse Anointing

Provision for the Nations

Joseph didn't just survive famine—he stewarded God's answer. He didn't merely interpret the times—he became provision for them.

"Let Pharaoh appoint commissioners... to collect all the food of the good years... so that the country may not be ruined by the famine" (Genesis 41:34–36).

This is the **storehouse anointing**: a call to carry provision—spiritual, emotional, and practical—for a world in need. It's not about hoarding for self-preservation, but positioning as a **conduit of Kingdom supply**. We are rivers in the wilderness, not reservoirs of fear.

"You open Your hand and satisfy the desire of every living thing" (Psalm 145:16).

Breaking the Poverty Spirit

You cannot build Kingdom storehouses with a poverty mindset. Poverty isn't just empty pockets—it's a spirit of fear that whispers scarcity and self-protection: *There's* never enough. *If I give, I'll lose. I need to protect what I have.*

But Heaven doesn't operate in lack. Yahweh is not El-Cheapo—He is **El Shaddai**, the All-Sufficient One.

The Word declares:

"The Lord is my shepherd; I shall not want" (Psalm 23:1).

"My God will supply all your needs according to His riches in glory" (Philippians 4:19).

"The blessing of the Lord makes one rich, and He adds no sorrow with it" (Proverbs 10:22).

"You will lend to many nations but borrow from none" (Deuteronomy 28:12).

"Give, and it will be given to you... pressed down, shaken together and running over" (Luke 6:38).

As I wrote in *Set Your Mind on Things Above the Sun,*

"Poverty is not broken by a bigger paycheck—it's broken by a renewed mind."

Joseph didn't wait for ideal conditions to build. He moved by revelation, preparing in wisdom before the famine ever struck. That's the Kingdom way—**we don't react to need; we respond to vision.** You are called to **steward provision with a Kingdom mindset,** rooted **in trust, not fear.**

A Lesson in Abundance

Years ago, I faced a season of financial strain. Bills were mounting, and fear whispered, *Hold back. Cut corners. Play it safe.* But Holy Spirit prompted me to sow into a friend on the mission field—one that had no way to repay me—and I obeyed.

I stood on this promise:

"And God is able to make all grace abound to you... so that in all things... you may abound in every good work" (2 Corinthians 9:8).

I sowed in faith, and Yahweh responded—not just with finances, but with wisdom, favor, and a supernatural peace that broke the fear of lack. That act didn't just meet a need—it broke a cycle.

Generosity is Heaven's economy. Giving is not loss—it's **seed in the ground**, destined to multiply.

Like Joseph, I learned that storehouses are built **through trust, not fear—by releasing, not withholding.**

You Are a Storehouse

Pharaoh sought *"a discerning and wise man"* to lead (Genesis 41:33). That's you.

Not a container, but a conduit.
Not a victim of lack, but a vessel of abundance.

The world doesn't need more consumers—it needs Kingdom **distributors**.
Storehouses are not built overnight. They're forged through **obedience, humility**, and **prophetic foresight**. Joseph's promotion wasn't flashy—it was faithful.

You carry not just provision, but **presence**.
Not just resources, but **revelation**.
Not just ideas, but **inheritance**.

After walking through the refining fire of relational loss and misrepresentation (Chapter 7), and learning to build as a son (Chapter 8), I've seen Yahweh rewire my understanding of provision.

I once lived in reaction—guarding resources out of survival. But the Lord shifted my sight. I am not the source—He is.

And when His Spirit flows through me, there is always more than enough.

This is the **Joseph anointing**:
Not to hoard, but to **heal**.
Not to **survive**, but to **serve**.
Not to **fear famine**, but to **feed it**.

The Storehouse Generation

God is raising sons and daughters right now—marked not by greed, but by **generosity, prophetic insight, and radical obedience**.

They are breaking generational cycles of debt and fear.
They are building systems of provision and discipleship.
They are preparing—not in panic, but in peace.

This is the Church Yahweh is birthing:
Not a building, but a blueprint.
Not a program, but a provision center for the hungry, hurting, and lost.

Famine Is a Setup for Provision

Joseph didn't cause the famine—but he interpreted it and prepared for it. That's what storehouses do. They don't retreat when the world shakes—they rise.

We are in a generation facing spiritual famine, emotional drought, and financial fear. But this is not the end—**it's our entrance**. Famine is not your fear—it's your *platform*.

You weren't born to survive scarcity—you were born to supply in it.
This is not just about wealth—it's about wells.
Wells of healing.
Wells of wisdom.
Wells of worship and Word.

"In the days of famine they will enjoy plenty" (Psalm 37:19).

Reflect and Act

My heart for you right now, as I speak into your life, is this: There's a part of you that knows you were made to break cycles of lack. You've tasted struggle—but you've also tasted Yahweh's sufficiency. The ache you feel when others go without? That's not just emotion—it's the storehouse anointing stirring within you. It's the Spirit inviting you to be a vessel of abundance in a world gripped by fear.

Reflect:
Where has fear of lack taken root?

Are you guarding what God gave you or stewarding it for others?

Act:
Take one step this week—sow time, wisdom, or resources.

Write down the areas you've withheld out of fear.

Repent. Release. Receive.

Declare aloud:

"I am not a slave to lack. I am a steward of abundance. I do not fear the famine—I prepare to feed it."

You are the answer someone is praying for.

Prayer of Provision and Breakthrough

Abba Father, Yahweh,
You define me not by earthly accounts but by the riches of Your Presence. With a yielded heart, I renounce the lie of lack and every fear of "not enough." Where a poverty mindset took root—through pain, history, or the prison of trials—I surrender it to You. Renew my mind to see through Heaven's eyes, above the sun.

Teach me to steward every resource—wisdom, wealth, influence, intimacy—with a son's heart and a servant's integrity. Heal any fear that clings to control or hoards in hesitation. Make me a storehouse, a vessel of healing, a channel of generosity, a refuge for those in famine.

Let the Joseph anointing rest on me: to discern what's ahead, prepare in wisdom, and provide for those You send. May what I carry sustain today and water generations yet to come.

Use me for Your glory. In the name of Yeshua, **Amen.**

Chapter 10: Above the Sun: Reigning from the Mountain Now

The Mountain of the Lord

"Come up here, and I will show you what must take place after this" (Revelation 4:1). You were never meant to live under the weight of this world—you were designed to reign above it, not in escape, but in authority. This isn't poetic language—*it's your spiritual inheritance as a son or daughter in Christ.* The Joseph anointing, forged through betrayal (*Chapter 7*), building (*Chapter 8*), and provision (*Chapter 9*), doesn't end in the palace—it ascends to the mountain of God's Presence.

Mountains are places of divine encounter. Moses received God's law on Sinai. Elijah heard Yahweh's whisper on Horeb. Jesus was transfigured on a mountain, revealing His glory. Now, in Christ, the invitation is yours: *"You have come to Mount Zion... the heavenly Jerusalem"* (Hebrews 12:22–23). You're not climbing to reach God—you're seated with Him now, *"raised up with Christ... in the heavenly realms"* (Ephesians 2:6).

The Secret Place: Your Seat of Dominion

The secret place isn't a refuge for retreat—it's your command center. *"He who dwells in the secret place of the Most High shall abide under the shadow of the Almighty"* (Psalm 91:1). You're not called to fight from the battlefield but to reign from the throne room. *Living above the sun* means dwelling here daily, not visiting when life overwhelms.

I know the weight of living *"under the sun"*—where betrayal, striving, and pressure feel relentless. Like Joseph, I've faced pits and prisons, feeling hidden and misunderstood. But in those seasons, Yahweh wasn't absent—He was preparing me on the mountain of His Presence. Through tears and silence, He taught me to see as He sees, to move by His Spirit, not my strength. The mountain isn't a place to hide—*it's where sons are revealed.*

Living Above the Sun

To live *above the sun* is to see life through eternal lenses, rising above accusation, offense, and fear. It's not denial—it's divine alignment; not fantasy, but Kingdom reality. Joseph lived this way, ruling with wisdom despite betrayal and famine (Genesis 41:46–49). You're called to do the same—not reacting to chaos, but reigning in Christ: *"In Him we live and move and have our being"* (Acts 17:28).

Reflect: Are you dwelling in the secret place or merely visiting? Have you forgotten what Yahweh whispered on the mountain in the valley's noise? He's calling you to return—not to strive, but to abide; not to perform, but to reign.

Write down the dreams, blueprints, and whispers He's given you. They're not imagination —they're instruction.

The Revealing of the Sons

"The creation waits in eager expectation for the children of God to be revealed" (Romans 8:19).

The Joseph anointing isn't just Joseph's story— it's a generation's mandate. The world's shaking isn't abandonment—it's the birth pangs of reformation. Yahweh isn't seeking perfect vessels, but prepared ones. You're not waiting for revival— *you're the answer to someone's famine.*

In my journey, I've seen this truth unfold. The years I felt invisible, watching others advance while I stood still, weren't rejection—*they were refinement.* Dreams died, only to be resurrected.

What the enemy meant for destruction, God turned for strength and compassion (Genesis 50:20). The Joseph anointing isn't a theory—it's my testimony, and it can be yours too.

From Hidden to Revealed

Joseph wasn't forgotten—*he was formed.* The pit was preparation, the prison was development, and the palace was his sudden assignment. If you've felt hidden or overlooked, know this: *obscurity is holy ground.* Yahweh is preparing you for impact in visibility. Your season of hiding is birthing authority for your revealing.

Sons and daughters aren't defined by platforms but by the Presence they carry. Joseph ruled Egypt as a son of Jacob, not an Egyptian. You're not called to conform to the world but to reveal the Kingdom: *"The Kingdom of God is not a matter of talk, but of power"* (1 Corinthians 4:20). True authority flows from identity, not crowns chased but crowns laid down.

A Reformation Movement

This isn't about brands or church models—it's a Kingdom mandate led by sons and daughters filled with Holy Spirit. Where famine reigns, we build storehouses. Where division festers, we forge bridges. Where fear grips, we bring freedom. Where survival lingers, we release strategy. You're not a spectator—*you're a son, a daughter, carrying reformation in your spirit.*

What blueprint has Yahweh shown you? What dream refuses to die? This is your moment to open the scroll, to forgive, to build, to reign. Let delays become destiny, scars become seeds, prisons become promotion.

Your Prophetic Declaration and Prayer

I am a son, a daughter, hidden but not forgotten, refined in the secret place for such a time as this. I live *above the sun*, dreaming with God, forgiving with courage, reigning with wisdom. I release provision, walk in identity, and carry reformation. I rise, not to be rescued, but to be revealed.

Abba Father, Yahweh, thank You for every test, tear, and triumph. You've anointed me, not abandoned me. I step into the Joseph anointing, saying yes to my scroll, yes to reformation. Reveal what's hidden in me, refine what's planted, and release Your dream through me. I am Yours, ready, revealed. In Yeshua's name, Amen.

Final Charge: Step Into the Scroll

Sons and daughters, the time is now. No more delay, fear, or hiding. The scroll is open, and you were born to lead in this shaking, not survive it. From the mountain of His Presence, release Heaven's vision. Reign from the secret place, letting the world see the Father's glory in you. This is the Joseph generation—rising, reforming, revealing His Kingdom.

Chapter 11: The Anointing That Abides

Sonship in a Fallen World

"My little children, I am writing these things to you so that you may not sin. But if anyone does sin, we have an Advocate with the Father, Jesus Christ the righteous" (1 John 2:1).

One morning, as 1 John 2–4 resonated in my spirit, I heard Yahweh whisper, *"The Joseph Anointing must be anchored in this."*

As I lingered in these words, they opened like a gate—a portal into the heart of the anointing. It's not just about dreams, delays, or destiny—it's about identity, intimacy, and immovability in Christ.

Joseph's power wasn't born in Pharaoh's palace but in a hidden life with God, guarded by purity, rooted in truth, and sustained by love. This is the anointing that abides, revealed in 1 John: a life shaped by Christ's advocacy, love's maturity, and discernment's protection in a fallen world.

Christ Our Advocate

Joseph stood alone in Potiphar's house, with no one to defend him against false accusations. No lawyer spoke for him in Pharaoh's prison. No brother pleaded his case when sold into slavery. Yet, he had an Advocate in Heaven: *"If anyone does sin, we have an Advocate with the Father— Jesus Christ the righteous"* (1 John 2:1). This truth is not abstract—it's deeply personal.

In seasons of being wounded by those I loved— facing twisted truths and silence (Chapter 7) —I learned this: Christ, my Advocate, intercedes for me. Like Joseph, I didn't need man's defense; Heaven pleaded for my maturity, turning pain into purpose. Joseph didn't defend himself; he lived in purity, trusting God to vindicate him.

"Whoever claims to live in Him must walk as Jesus did" (1 John 2:6).

The Joseph anointing aligns our walk with Christ's—blameless, forgiving, set apart— empowering us to stand firm in adversity.

The New Commandment: Love One Another

Love was the dividing line in Joseph's story. His brothers lacked it, consumed by envy. Potiphar's wife counterfeited it, driven by lust. Pharaoh witnessed its fruit in Joseph's wisdom. And Joseph embodied it, weeping with those who betrayed him (Genesis 45:14–15).

John calls this a *"new commandment"* that is both ancient and renewed: to love one another in truth.

"Whoever loves his brother abides in the light, and in him there is no cause for stumbling" (1 John 2:10).

The Joseph anointing matures in love's response to betrayal. Do we choose light or resentment? Love or pain's reaction? In my journey, forgiving those who twisted my story wasn't optional—it was proof of abiding in Christ.

Love is the mantle's mark, tested not in dungeons but in our hearts toward those who wound us.

Reflect: Who has God called you to love through betrayal? Choose light, and let love anchor your anointing.

Do Not Love the World

Joseph lived in Egypt, but Egypt never lived in him. *"Do not love the world or the things in the world... The world is passing away along with its desires, but whoever does the will of God abides forever"* (1 John 2:15, 17).

He wore Pharaoh's ring yet carried Yahweh's Spirit, ruling a corrupt system without bowing to its gods. The abiding anointing refuses to blend in, even in elevation.

To carry the Joseph anointing, you must reign in this world without being ruled by it. Manage kingdoms, but guard your worship. Build storehouses (*Chapter 9*), but never trade your soul for their keys. Living above the sun (*Chapter 10*) means walking in authority without idolizing visibility, loving without compromise. You're called to lead with wisdom, not conform to the world's desires, standing firm as Joseph did in a fallen land.

The Manifestation of the Sons

"See what great love the Father has lavished on us, that we should be called children of God! And that is what we are!" (1 John 3:1).

Joseph was hidden not by chance but by divine identity. The world didn't recognize him because it didn't know God. Pharaoh saw not a slave but the Spirit of God (Genesis 41:38). Joseph didn't announce himself—he was revealed.

The world groans for sons and daughters, not personalities (*Romans 8:19*). Like Joseph, you're refined in hidden places, not recruited for stages.

In my seasons of obscurity, I felt invisible, but Yahweh was forging sonship. My identity isn't man's approval—*it's Heaven's affirmation*. You don't need to explain your process to those absent from your becoming. Your revealing comes from the Father's love, not public favor.

Love That Reforms

"Dear friends, let us love one another, for love comes from God... God is love" (1 John 4:7–8).

Joseph could have ruled with revenge, but he chose restoration, embracing those who sold him (Genesis 45:4–5). His love wasn't weakness—it was fullness, modeled after Christ. *"We love because He first loved us"* (1 John 4:19).

Mature love reforms, not retaliates. It feeds betrayers, weeps with wounds, and breaks bread in brokenness. In my betrayal, I learned to love forward, not from scarcity but from God's abundance. Who are you called to forgive publicly for private pain? What relationships or systems is God asking you to heal through love? Your capacity to love in adversity is Heaven's measure of maturity.

A Spirit of Truth and Discernment

"By this you know the Spirit of God: Every spirit that confesses Jesus Christ has come in the flesh is from God" (1 John 4:2).

Joseph's power lay not just in interpretation but in discernment—knowing God's voice from man's manipulation. He read Pharaoh's dream, his brothers' hearts, and the moment for reconciliation (Genesis 41:25–28; 45:1–3). You, too, must walk in this: not reaction, but revelation; not fear, but truth.

The world's spirit deceives, trading holiness for hype. But the abiding anointing teaches and guards against counterfeits (1 John 2:27). As a reformer and watchman (*Chapter 10*), you stand between chaos and strategy, famine and provision.

Reflect: Are you reacting to voices or discerning the Spirit? Where is God calling you to speak truth, even at personal cost? The Joseph anointing equips you to lead with clarity in a clouded world.

Final Charge: The Josephs Are Rising

The anointing that abides endures—unflickering under pressure, unshaken by praise. Joseph's life—betrayed, buried, raised, revealed—mirrors Christ's pattern, a prophetic blueprint for you.

You're not building monuments to self (*Chapter 8*) but stewarding movements for the Kingdom (*Chapter 9*). This world isn't your home; its applause isn't your inheritance. You live above the sun (*Chapter 10*), walking in purity, love, and truth.

This is the hour of unveiling. As 1 John declares, we have an Advocate in Christ (1 John 2:1), calling you out of hiding into revealing.

Declare in your spirit: I am anointed, and the anointing abides. I walk as Christ walked, loving with maturity, forgiving with courage, discerning with clarity. The Father's love defines me, His Word refines me, His Spirit leads me. I reveal the Kingdom, hidden no longer.

Prayer of Alignment

Yahweh, thank You for the anointing that abides, rooted in Your unchanging love. I praise You for Yeshua—my Advocate, Savior, and pattern. Today, I receive Your love afresh, aligning with Heaven's perspective above the sun. I renounce the world's patterns and every false identity, including those forged in the prison of betrayal. I choose to walk as a son—pure, bold, discerning, true.

Spirit of Truth, guard my mind. Spirit of Love, guide my steps. Let Christ's life shine through me. I forgive those who've betrayed me, love those who've wounded me, and discern Your voice above all. I am Yours, ready, revealed.

Amen.

Conclusion: You Are the Fulfillment of the Dream

What began as a whisper in the night has become a roar of destiny. Joseph's journey was never about mere elevation—it was about preservation, not just authority but alignment with Heaven's heart. His dreams weren't fantasies; they were divine forecasts—blueprints waiting to be fulfilled through process, pain, and purity. Having embraced the anointing that abides in love and truth (Chapter 11), you're now called to fulfill the dream, carrying Joseph's mantle into reformation. As this book closes, the mantle of the Joseph anointing doesn't rest on a shelf. It rests on you.

The Dream Has Found a Vessel

You're not merely reading history—you're stepping into prophecy. Like the young Joseph, misunderstood yet marked (Chapter 1), you've carried a Kingdom mindset through pain (Chapter 3). Joseph's dreams of stars and sheaves were about legacy, forgiveness, provision, and the revealing of sons (Romans 8:19).

Through every chapter—from the pit (Chapter 7) to the palace— you've seen your own reflection: God preparing you in hiddenness, promoting you through humility, and positioning you for purposes beyond your own strength. In my seasons of being wounded by others (Chapter 7), I discovered this truth: the dream isn't just a story to admire—it's a calling to continue. You are not just living Joseph's story—you are its next chapter.

From Revelation to Reformation

These pages haven't delivered a message to applaud but a blueprint to embody. *"The word tested him until the time came for its fulfillment"* (Psalm 105:19). You've been equipped to:

- Carry dreams through seasons of delay (Chapter 7).
- Walk in purity when no one sees (Chapter 8).
- Forgive those who wound you deeply (Chapter 11).
- Lead with wisdom forged in fire (Chapter 9).
- Reign without losing sonship (Chapter 10).

- Dwell above the sun, unshaken by storms (Chapter 3). This isn't information—it's impartation. Like Joseph, you're called to turn revelation into reformation, building what Heaven has shown you for a world in need (Matthew 5:14–16).

You Are the One

A famine grips the land—spiritual, emotional, and physical—and Yahweh is raising Josephs. Not just preachers, but intercessors; not just authors, but apostolic architects; not just survivors, but storehouse builders (Chapter 9).

Your obedience matters.

Your voice carries weight.

Every delay was divine, every silence sacred, every heartbreak a chisel in Heaven's hands.

In my journey, I felt the weight of hiddenness and family silence (Chapter 5), wondering if my wounds would define me.

But God was shaping me, as He is shaping you, to fulfill His dream.

You're no longer just a dreamer—you're the vessel of its fulfillment.

The testing is passing.

The revealing is beginning.

You carry the Joseph anointing—not for fame, but for famine; not for self, but for those who will draw from your storehouses.

The Six Prophetic Pillars of the Joseph Anointing

These six pillars form the blueprint of Joseph's journey— and yours as a son or daughter called to the Joseph anointing:

Dreamer – Receiving the Divine Blueprint *(Genesis 37:5–11)*

Dreams awaken destiny before maturity. Joseph's visions were not earned but inherited, igniting his identity (Chapter 1). Your dreams from Heaven are God's whispers of what's to come. Guard them in faith.

Son – Identity Before Assignment *(Genesis 37:3–4)*

Joseph's strength was rooted in sonship, not dreams alone. Before you rule, rest in your identity as a beloved child. Sonship carries favor through relationship, not performance (1 John 3:1).

Servant – Humility in Hiddenness *(Genesis 39:1–6)*

Authority is forged in faithfulness. In Potiphar's house, Joseph served without recognition, building a heart free from pride (Chapter 3). Your unseen obedience prepares you for visible impact.

Prisoner – Processed by Pain (*Genesis 39:20–23*)

The prison kills entitlement and deepens trust. Joseph's ministry to others in confinement revealed hope's power in hiddenness (Chapter 7). Pain is your classroom of surrender.

Prophet – Speaking with Discernment and Authority (*Genesis 41:14–16*)

The prophetic mantle brings strategy, not just revelation. Joseph interpreted Pharaoh's dream with Heaven's wisdom (Chapter 11). Your voice must carry solutions, not just insight.

Governor – Ruling from a Redeemed Heart (*Genesis 41:41–57*)

Joseph ruled with mercy, stewarding provision for nations. This pillar is the fruit of formation—authority that blesses generations, not just moments (Chapter 9).

These pillars aren't a ladder but a cycle of formation, revisited as you grow into a reformer, a son, a vessel of Kingdom provision. Welcome to the Joseph anointing. Live above the sun (Chapter 10).

Final Prophetic Charge

You didn't stumble into this moment—you were sent. Every wound, delay, promotion, and promise led here. The scroll is open. Step into the secret place (*Chapter 10*) and ask Yahweh:

- What have You written in my scroll for this season? Listen. See His blueprint.
- What must I forgive, finish, or release to walk in it? Let go of offense's baggage (Chapter 11).
- Where have I been hiding when I should be building? Rise, don't shrink (Chapter 8).

Reflect: What dream has God rekindled through these pages? Write it down, and declare His faithfulness. Stand and proclaim: *I am not just part of the story. I am the next chapter.*

You were born for reformation. You're held in Heaven's hands, formed for eternal purpose. The Josephs are rising. The storehouses are opening.

The scrolls are unrolling. Take your mantle. Build what Heaven has shown you.

Final Commissioning Prayer

Father, I thank You for calling me for such a time as this. Thank You for entrusting me with dreams, assignments, and scrolls. I repent for every fear that delayed me. I forgive those who wounded me (Chapter 7). I release those who misjudged me. I step fully into my mantle as a son.

Let the Joseph anointing rest on me—pure, unshakable, revealed. Turn every pit into redemption, every scar into seed, every delay into destiny. Use my life to preserve, protect, and prepare. Reveal Yourself through me. In Yeshua's name, Amen.

Appendix: Deeper Reflections

These reflections invite you to linger in the revelation of Joseph's story and its parallels to your own journey. Born from the fire of personal experience and the truth of Scripture, they deepen your understanding of betrayal, redemption, and reigning in God's Presence. Pause here. Reflect. Let Holy Spirit speak into your wounds as you consider how God is turning your pit into a platform.

Reflections from the Pit: Insights on Betrayal and Redemption

What Did Benjamin Think?

When Joseph stood before his brothers in Egypt and declared, *"You intended to harm me, but God intended it for good"* (Genesis 50:20), I often wonder: What did Benjamin think? Unlike his brothers, Benjamin hadn't been part of the betrayal. He didn't throw Joseph into the pit or dip his coat in blood. He grew up under the shadow of a lie, believing his older brother was dead, shaped by a narrative of loss and silence. Imagine the moment. Joseph, alive and ruling

Egypt, reveals himself. The brothers who betrayed him stand guilty, but Benjamin stands in shock. Confusion, grief, and relief must have swirled in his heart. What was it like to realize the brothers he loved had buried the truth? To learn that while he wept for Joseph, they carried a secret?

Yet Joseph didn't expose them—not even to Benjamin. He could have unmasked their betrayal before Pharaoh's court, demanding a public confession. But *Genesis 45:1 tells us* that *"Joseph could not restrain himself before all those who stood by him, and he cried out, 'Make everyone go out from me!'"* What happened next wasn't just emotional—it was intentional. Joseph cleared the room—shielding his brothers from shame and guarding Benjamin's innocence. This act of mercy didn't excuse their sin—it preserved their dignity. More than that, it preserved the possibility of reconciliation. Joseph chose to cover what God still intended to redeem.

Reflection: Have you ever discovered a hidden truth that reshaped your understanding of your family or community? How does Joseph's choice to cover his brothers' sin challenge you to respond to those who've hurt you? Take a moment to ask

Holy Spirit to reveal where you can choose mercy over exposure, guarding what God desires to redeem.

The Pain of Exposure

Betrayal stings deepest from those who know us best. I've experienced moments where a restored chapter of my story was misunderstood, causing deep relational strain. But Yahweh taught me the power of mercy over exposure. Like Joseph, I covered the wounds, trusting God to redeem my legacy with His truth. In those moments, I wanted to defend myself, to set the record straight.

But God taught me a harder lesson: Anyone can expose a wound; only the healed can cover a legacy. This is what Joseph understood in Egypt— that vindication isn't as powerful as redemption. Healing gave him eyes to see his brothers not as enemies, but as part of God's greater plan. Covering them didn't excuse their sin; it preserved the future. Sometimes, healing means we stop rehearsing the betrayal—and start protecting the legacy.

Joseph's brothers dipped his coat in blood to craft a false narrative. Today's "bloody coat" might look like a social media post or a whispered rumor. But God's truth outlasts every lie. *He redeems what's been twisted and restores what's been broken.*

When Joseph cleared the room in Genesis 45—removing witnesses before revealing himself—he wasn't just protecting his brothers from shame. He was protecting *his family's future* from being defined by that shame. That's what healed people do. They cover what God intends to restore, because they see from the mountain—not the pit.

Reflection: Where have you felt the sting of exposure or a distorted narrative? How has God met you in that pain? Write down one lie spoken over you, and ask God to replace it with His truth, trusting Him to be your Defender.

Where is God calling you to cover instead of expose? Can you trust Him to be your vindication while you walk in mercy?

Breaking the Curse of Betrayal

Betrayal doesn't just wound—it seeks to define. But God's plans cannot be cancelled. In the wilderness of my own betrayal, I stood at a crossroads. I could have exposed the distortion, weaponized the truth to fight back. Instead, I heard Holy Spirit's whisper: *"Will you build an altar of forgiveness where pain once ruled?"* In that moment, I declared over my family line:

The curse of exposure ends here. The spirit of Jezebel will not define my legacy. Mercy will rewrite our story. Restoration will find our children's children.

I chose to break agreement with bitterness and align with God's redemptive purpose. What was meant for evil, God turned for good—just as He did for Joseph.

This is the Joseph anointing: to live above the sun, above the lies, the betrayal, and the pain. It's choosing to serve while bleeding, to prophesy while longing, and to trust when hope seems lost. The wilderness isn't your end—it's where God forges your voice, refines your character, and prepares you for a legacy that outlives the pit.

Reflection and Prayer: Where in your life do you need to break the curse of betrayal? Speak this declaration aloud: *"I am not disqualified. I am not forgotten. I am being refined. What was meant for evil, God will turn for good. My wounds will become wells of life for others."* Ask Holy Spirit to show you one step toward forgiveness or restoration today.

Selah: The pit, the prison, the palace—each is a chapter in God's story for you. As A.W. Tozer wrote, *"It is doubtful whether God can bless a man greatly until He has hurt him deeply."* Your pain is not wasted. It's the raw material of your purpose. Let God meet you in the fire, and watch Him turn your wounds into wells of healing for others.

Reflections from the Mountain: Insights on Reigning Above the Sun

Encounters on the Mountain

Mountains are sacred spaces where God meets His people. Moses ascended Mount Sinai to receive the law, trembling at Yahweh's voice (Exodus 19:18–20). Elijah, weary and hunted, found God's whisper on Mount Horeb, restoring his purpose (1 Kings 19:11–12). Jesus, on the mount of transfiguration, revealed His glory, inviting three disciples into divine encounter (Matthew 17:1–3). These moments weren't reserved for the elite—they foreshadow your inheritance: a seat on Mount Zion, the heavenly Jerusalem (Hebrews 12:22–23). In my seasons of being betrayed and hiding, I found my own mountain—the secret place where Yahweh spoke identity over me. When I felt invisible, He whispered, *"You are not forgotten."* When I questioned my calling, He unrolled blueprints that burned with eternal purpose. The mountain isn't a place to hide—it's where sons and daughters are formed for reformation.

Reflection: Recall a "mountain" moment when God met you in His Presence. What did He whisper? Write it down, and ask Holy Spirit to renew its clarity for this season.

Living Above the Noise

Living above the sun means rising above the noise of this world—accusation, pressure, and performance. It's refusing to descend into fear or retreat under the valley's weight. I know this struggle. In the pits and prisons of my journey, I lived "under the sun," where everything felt heavy and urgent. Striving left me weary, as if my efforts were never enough. But Yahweh called me higher—to dwell in the secret place, not just visit when life overwhelmed (Psalm 91:1). The secret place is your command center, where you see as God sees and move by His Spirit. It's not a Sunday escape—it's your daily habitation. There, I learned to silence the clamor of striving and tune my heart to His voice. The dreams and scrolls He gave me weren't imagination—they were instruction, calling me to reign with revelation, not reaction.

Reflection: Where have you felt the weight of living "under the sun"? Identify one area (e.g., fear, striving) and declare: *"I live above the sun, in the flow of Your revelation, not the weight of my pressure."* Ask God to draw you back to the secret place today.

Opening Your Scroll

The Joseph anointing is a call to open the scroll of God's blueprint for your life. In my hidden years, I questioned the silence, wondering if I'd missed my calling. But every delay was destiny, every scar a seed. Like Joseph, I was refined in obscurity for impact in visibility (Genesis 41:46–49). The world groans for what you carry: *"The creation waits in eager expectation for the children of God to be revealed"* (Romans 8:19). Your scroll isn't about platforms—it's about Presence, not crowns chased but crowns laid down at His feet.

Prayer: *Abba Father, open the scroll of my life. Reveal the dreams, blueprints, and whispers You've entrusted to me. Forgive where I've descended into fear or striving. Align my heart with Your voice, and let me reign from the mountain with wisdom and courage. I am Your son, Your daughter, ready to be revealed. In Yeshua's name, Amen.*

Selah: The mountain is your home. Every pit, prison, and delay has prepared you for this moment. As you dwell in the secret place, let Yahweh's whisper become your roar, releasing reformation through your life.

Scriptural Bibliography

Below is a comprehensive list of all Bible passages referenced in the manuscript, organized by book, chapter, and verse, with their respective versions as specified or inferred from the text.

Genesis 37:5–11 (NKJV)): Joseph's dreams (Chapter 1, page 8)

5 Now Joseph had a dream, and he told it to his brothers; and they hated him even more. 6 So he said to them, "Please hear this dream which I have dreamed: 7 There we were, binding sheaves in the field. Then behold, my sheaf arose and also stood upright; and indeed your sheaves stood all around and bowed down to my sheaf." 8 And his brothers said to him, "Shall you indeed reign over us? Or shall you indeed have dominion over us?" So they hated him even more for his dreams and for his words. 9 Then he dreamed still another dream and told it to his brothers, and said, "Look, I have dreamed another dream. And this time, the sun, the moon, and the eleven stars bowed down to me." 10 So he told it to his father and his brothers; and his father rebuked him and said to him, "What is this dream that you have dreamed? Shall your mother and I and your brothers indeed come to bow down to the earth before you?" 11 And his brothers envied him, but his father kept the matter in mind.

Genesis 39:2–4 (NKJV): Lord with Joseph in Potiphar's house (Chapter 2, page 15)

2 The Lord was with Joseph, and he was a successful man; and he was in the house of his master the Egyptian. 3 And his master saw that the Lord was with him and that the Lord made all he did to prosper in his hand. 4 So Joseph found favor in his sight, and served him. Then he made him overseer of his house, and all that he had he put under his authority.

Genesis 39:21–23 (ESV): Lord with Joseph in prison (Chapter 4, page 29)

21 But the Lord was with Joseph and showed him steadfast love and gave him favor in the sight of the keeper of the prison. 22 And the keeper of the prison put Joseph in charge of all the prisoners who were in the prison. Whatever was done there, he was the one who did it. 23 The keeper of the prison paid no attention to anything that was in Joseph's charge, because the Lord was with him. And whatever he did, the Lord made it succeed.

Genesis 40:8 (NKJV): Interpretations belong to God (Chapter 4, page 31)

8 And they said to him, 'We each have had a dream, and there is no interpreter of it.' So Joseph said to them, 'Do not interpretations belong to God? Tell them to me, please.'

Genesis 41:16 (NIV): God gives Pharaoh an answer (Chapter 6, page 45)

16 'I cannot do it,' Joseph replied to Pharaoh, 'but God will give Pharaoh the answer he desires.'

Genesis 41:25–36(NKJV): Joseph's interpretation and plan (Chapter 8, page 67).

25 Then Joseph said to Pharaoh, 'The dreams of Pharaoh are one; God has shown Pharaoh what He is about to do: 26 The seven good cows are seven years, and the seven good heads are

seven years; the dreams are one. 27 And the seven thin and ugly cows which came up after them are seven years, and the seven empty heads blighted by the east wind are seven years of famine. 28 This is the thing which I have spoken to Pharaoh. God has shown Pharaoh what He is about to do. 29 Indeed seven years of great plenty will come throughout all the land of Egypt; 30 but after them seven years of famine will arise, and all the plenty will be forgotten in the land of Egypt; and the famine will deplete the land. 31 So the plenty will not be known in the land because of the famine following, for it will be very severe. 32 And the dream was repeated to Pharaoh twice because the thing is established by God, and God will shortly bring it to pass. 33 Now therefore, let Pharaoh select a discerning and wise man, and set him over the land of Egypt. 34 Let Pharaoh do this, and let him appoint officers over the land, to collect one-fifth of the produce of the land of Egypt in the seven plentiful years. 35 And let them gather all the food of those good years that are coming, and store up grain under the authority of Pharaoh, and let them keep food in the cities. 36 Then that food shall be as a reserve for the land for the seven years of famine which shall be in the land of Egypt, that the land may not perish during the famine.'

Genesis 45:5–8 (NKJV): Joseph's purpose for preservation (Chapter 9, page 78)

5 But now, do not therefore be grieved or angry with yourselves because you sold me here; for God sent me before you to preserve life. 6 For these two years the famine has been in the land, and there are still five years in which there will be neither plowing nor harvesting. 7 And God sent me before you to preserve a posterity for you in the earth, and to save your lives by a great deliverance. 8 So now it was not you who sent me here, but God; and He has made me a father to Pharaoh, and lord of all his house, and a ruler throughout all the land of Egypt.

Genesis 50:20 (AMPC): God meant it for good (Chapter 7, page 56; Appendix, page 112)

As for you, you thought evil against me, but God meant it for good, to bring about that many people should be kept alive, as they are this day.

Exodus 20:12 (NKJV): Honor your father and mother (Chapter 2, page 17)

Honor your father and your mother, that your days may be long upon the land which the Lord your God is giving you.

Deuteronomy 8:18 (NKJV): God gives power to get wealth (Chapter 9, page 79)

And you shall remember the Lord your God, for it is He who gives you power to get wealth, that He may establish His covenant which He swore to your fathers, as it is this day.

1 Samuel 16:7 (NIV): Man looks at outward appearance (Chapter 3, page 22)

But the Lord said to Samuel, "Do not consider his appearance or his height, for I have rejected him. The Lord does not look at the things people look at. People look at the outward appearance, but the Lord looks at the heart."

Psalm 1:1–3 (NKJV): Blessed is the man (Chapter 10, page 89)

1 Blessed is the man who walks not in the counsel of the ungodly, nor stands in the path of sinners, nor sits in the seat of the scornful; 2 But his delight is in the law of the Lord, and in His law he meditates day and night. 3 He shall be like a tree planted by the rivers of water, that brings forth its fruit in its season, whose leaf also shall not wither; and whatever he does shall prosper.

Psalm 23:1 (NKJV): The Lord is my shepherd (Chapter 9, page 77).

The Lord is my shepherd; I shall not want.

Psalm 105:17–19 (NKJV): Joseph tested until his word came (Chapter 5, page 38).

He sent a man before them—Joseph—who was sold as a slave. They hurt his feet with fetters, he was laid in irons. Until the time that his word came to pass, the word of the Lord tested him.

Proverbs 3:5–6 (NKJV): Trust in the Lord (Chapter 8, page 66).

Trust in the Lord with all your heart, and lean not on your own understanding; in all your ways acknowledge Him, and He shall direct your paths.

Proverbs 22:29 (NKJV): Diligent man before kings (Chapter 2, page 16).

Do you see a man who excels in his work? He will stand before kings; he will not stand before unknown men.

Isaiah 55:8–9 (NKJV): My thoughts are higher (Chapter 10, page 90).

"For My thoughts are not your thoughts, nor are your ways My ways," says the Lord. "For as the heavens are higher than the earth, so are My ways higher than your ways, and My thoughts than your thoughts."

Jeremiah 29:11 (NIV): Plans to prosper you (Introduction, page 4).

"For I know the plans I have for you," declares the Lord, "plans to prosper you and not to harm you, plans to give you hope and a future."

Daniel 1:17 (NKJV): God gave knowledge and skill (Chapter 8, page 68).

As for these four young men, God gave them knowledge and skill in all literature and wisdom; and Daniel had understanding in all visions and dreams.

Matthew 6:33 (NKJV): Seek first the Kingdom (Chapter 9, page 80).

But seek first the kingdom of God and His righteousness, and all these things shall be added to you.

John 15:5 (NKJV): Apart from Me, you can do nothing (Chapter 11, page 98).

5 "I am the vine, you are the branches. He who abides in Me, and I in him, bears much fruit; for without Me you can do nothing."

John 16:33 (NLT): I have overcome the world (Chapter 7, page 55).

33 "I have told you all this so that you may have peace in me. Here on earth you will have many trials and sorrows. But take heart, because I have overcome the world."

Romans 8:28 (NKJV): All things work together for good (Chapter 7, page 57; Appendix, page 113).

28 And we know that all things work together for good to those who love God, to those who are the called according to His purpose.

Romans 12:2 (NKJV): Renewing of your mind (Chapter 9, page 76).

2 And do not be conformed to this world, but be transformed by the renewing of your mind, that you may prove what is that good and acceptable and perfect will of God.

2 Corinthians 4:18 (NKJV): Things unseen are eternal (Chapter 10, page 91).

18 while we do not look at the things which are seen, but at the things which are not seen. For the things which are seen are temporary, but the things which are not seen are eternal.

Ephesians 2:6 (NKJV): Seated in heavenly places (Chapter 10, page 88).

6 and raised us up together, and made us sit together in the heavenly places in Christ Jesus,

Ephesians 3:20 (NKJV): Able to do exceedingly (Preface, page 2).

20 Now to Him who is able to do exceedingly abundantly above all that we ask or think, according to the power that works in us,

Philippians 3:13–14 (NKJV): Press toward the goal (Chapter 6, page 46).

13 Brethren, I do not count myself to have apprehended; but one thing I do, forgetting those things which are behind and reaching forward to those things which are ahead,
14 I press toward the goal for the prize of the upward call of God in Christ Jesus.

Colossians 3:2 (NKJV): Set your mind on things above (Chapter 8, page 65; Chapter 10, page 87).

2 Set your mind on things above, not on things on the earth.

Hebrews 12:1–2 (ESV): Run with endurance (Chapter 11, page 99).

1 Therefore, since we are surrounded by so great a cloud of witnesses, let us also lay aside every weight, and sin which clings so closely, and let us run with endurance the race that is set before us, 2 looking to Jesus, the founder and perfecter of our faith, who for the joy that was set before him endured the cross, despising the shame, and is seated at the right hand of the throne of God.

James 1:2–4 (NKJV): Count it all joy (Chapter 5, page 39).

2 My brethren, count it all joy when you fall into various trials, 3 knowing that the testing of your faith produces patience. 4 But let patience have its perfect work, that you may be perfect and complete, lacking nothing.

1 John 3:1 (NIV): What great love (Chapter 11, page 97).

1 See what great love the Father has lavished on us, that we should be called children of God! And that is what we are! The reason the world does not know us is that it did not know him.

1 Thessalonians 5:23 (NKJV) (Chapter 11 & Conclusion)

"Now may the God of peace Himself sanctify you completely; and may your whole spirit, soul, and body be preserved blameless..."

Acts 17:28 (NKJV) (Conclusion)

"For in Him we live and move and have our being..."

1 Kings 19:12 (NKJV)

"...a still small voice."

Isaiah 61:3 (NKJV) (Chapter 7)

"...to give them beauty for ashes, the oil of joy for mourning..."

Philippians 4:13 (NKJV) (Chapter 11)

"I can do all things through Christ who strengthens me."

About The Author

Eric D. Cooper is a prophetic voice, visionary leader, and reformer whose life has been shaped by fire, tested by truth, and anchored in unwavering hope.

With over four decades of experience in business, ministry, leadership, and mentorship, Eric carries a distinctive Joseph anointing—refined in the pit, forged in the prison, and commissioned for reformation. His journey from hiddenness to authority is marked by deep surrender, supernatural wisdom, and a passion for guiding others into their Kingdom identity.

Eric's writing blends Biblical wisdom, practical insights, and profound spiritual truths, igniting a desire for holiness, sonship, and authentic partnership with Yahweh's design. His compassionate leadership has empowered countless individuals to navigate life's challenges with resilience and purpose, leaving a legacy of transformation across generations. As the founder of Above the Sun Consultant Group and co-leader of a reformation movement, Eric champions presence over performance, transformation over tradition, and legacy over popularity.

In a world filled with noise, Eric's work stands as a beacon, calling sons and daughters to live above the sun, anchored in truth, and walking in the fullness of their divine calling.

Invitation To Connect

If this book has stirred something deep in your spirit—if you've wept, wrestled, or awakened to fresh purpose—then I want you to know: this journey doesn't end with the last page.

I'd be honored to hear your story.

Whether you're walking through a pit, rising from a prison, or standing at the threshold of purpose, your voice matters. This message of reformation is not just a book—it's a movement of sons and daughters stepping into their God-given destiny. And I believe you're one of them.

Let's stay connected. Let's grow together. Let's keep dreaming— *above the sun.*

You can find new teachings, prophetic insights, and ministry updates at:

- www.TheJosephAnointing.com
- www.ericcooper.com
- Email: contact@ericcooper.com
- Instagram: @abovethesunbooks
- Facebook: @EricCooperAuthor

You were born for reformation. Let's walk it out—together.

With honor,

Eric D. Cooper

Books by Eric D. Cooper

Set Your Mind on Things Above the Sun

How to Develop a Kingdom Mindset

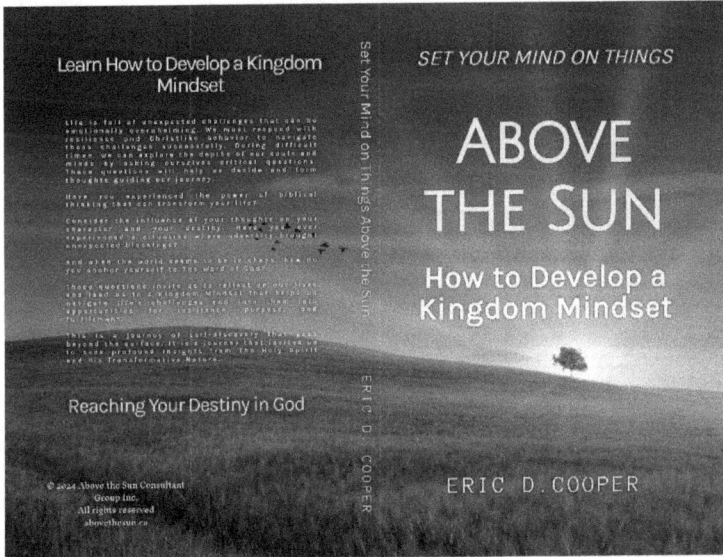

Available in English, Spanish, and Portuguese

A transformative journey into intentional focus and spiritual empowerment, equipping readers with Biblical principles to live a purpose-driven life rooted in a Kingdom mindset.

I Am Mad at Hell—I'm Not Taking It Anymore!

Unveiling the Truths of Spiritual Warfare and Personal Empowerment

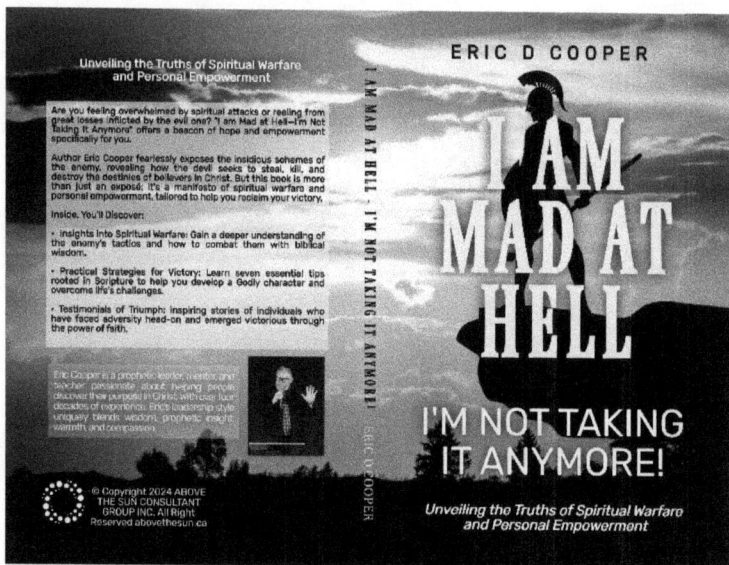

Available in English and Spanish

A bold guide to overcoming spiritual attacks and adversity through faith, offering practical strategies and inspiring testimonies to live a victorious life.

The Journey of Restoration

Rediscovering Hope in the Midst of Chaos – A Modern-Day Allegory

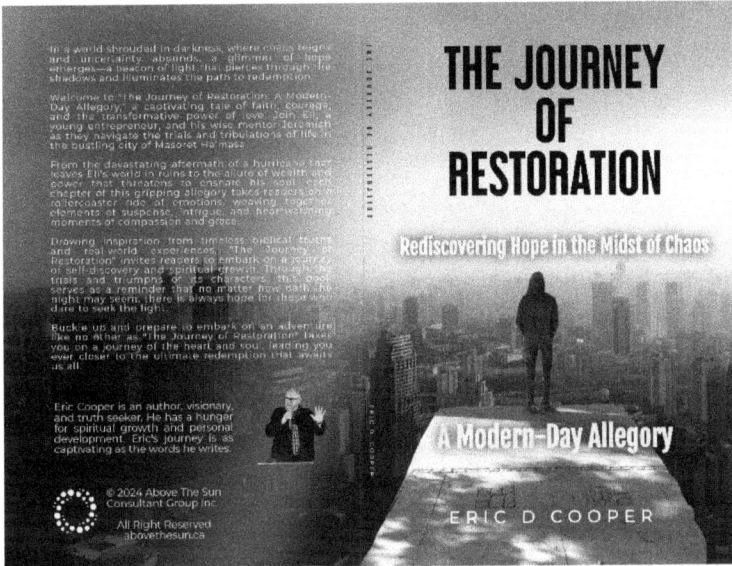

Available in English

A compelling Biblical allegory following Eli's journey through trials in Masoret Ha'masa, reflecting themes of resilience, redemption, and hope.

Restoration Journey

A Daily Guide to Rebuilding Your Relationship with God through the Psalms and Proverbs

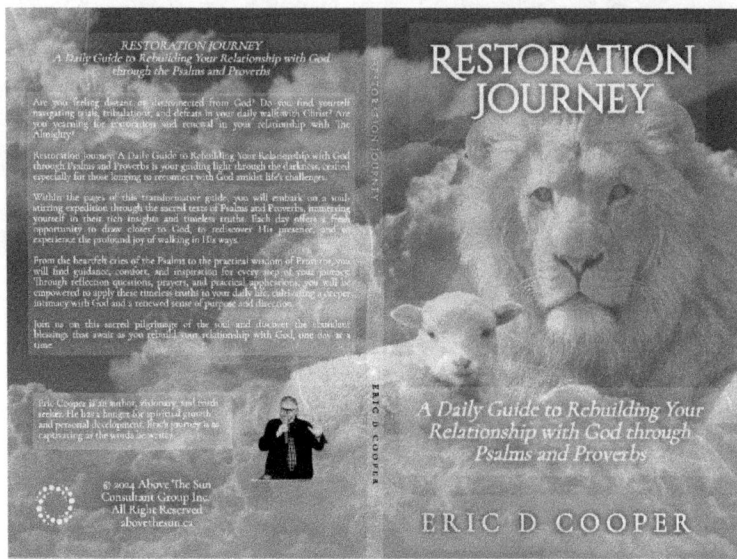

Available in English, Spanish, and Portuguese

A 30-day devotional guiding readers through Psalms and Proverbs to renew their relationship with God, with reflections, prayers, and practical applications.

Aprenda Como Desenvolver uma
Mentalidade do Reino

SUA MENTE NAS COISAS

O que quer que você toque, você cria espaço para
- O que quer que você tema, você empodera!
Desenvolver uma Mentalidade do Reino e andar
no poder sobrenatural do Espírito Santo requer
fazer escolhas Divinas, especialmente quando
enfrentamos tempos difíceis e desafios. A chave
para alcançar isso é focar nas coisas acima do
sol! Estamos familiarizados com o Espírito Santo
que habita em nós - Aquele que vive nos
corações de cada crente. Embora esta seja uma
verdade incrível, a plenitude desta realidade é
mais significativa do que podemos imaginar!

- Você se sente sobrecarregado pelas
constantes demandas da sua vida cotidiana?

- Você está em busca de respostas para as
questões mais profundas da vida?

Se sim, você não está sozinho. Muitos de nós
lutamos para encontrar o equilíbrio certo entre
nossas ambições mundanas e nossos valores
espirituais. Pode ser desafiador navegar pelos
ecos da vida e manter nosso senso de propósito e
direção. Desbloqueie o poder do seu espírito e
descubra a sabedoria eterna dentro de você. Esta
livre o sobre superar desafios e equipar-se com
uma Mentalidade do Reino e as ferramentas
necessárias para viver uma vida plena em Cristo.

Alcançando Seu Destino em Deus

ACIMA
DO SOL

Como Desenvolver uma
Mentalidade do Reino

ERIC D. COOPER

Tradução por Luanna Monteiro

Coloque Sua Mente nas Coisas Acima do Sol

ERIC D. COOPER

Cover 1 — Más Allá del Sol

Back cover

Aprende a Desarrollar una Mentalidad del Reino

La vida está llena de desafíos inesperados que pueden ser emocionalmente abrumadores. Debemos responder con resiliencia y un comportamiento semejante a Cristo para navegar exitosamente estos desafíos. Durante los tiempos difíciles, podemos explorar las profundidades de nuestras almas y mentes haciéndonos preguntas críticas. Estas preguntas nos ayudarán a decidir y formar pensamientos que guían nuestro camino.

¿Has experimentado el poder del pensamiento bíblico que puede transformar tu vida?

Considera la influencia de tus pensamientos en tu estado y tu destino. ¿Alguna vez has experimentado una situación en la que la adversidad trajo resultados inesperados?

Y cuando el mundo parece estar en caos, ¿cómo te enfocas en la Palabra de Dios?

Estas preguntas nos invitan a reflexionar sobre nuestras vidas y nos conducen a una mentalidad del reino que nos ayuda a enfrentar los desafíos de la vida y convertirla en oportunidades de crecimiento, propósito y claridad.

Este es un viaje de autodescubrimiento que va más allá de lo superficial. Es un viaje que nos invita a buscar un profundo conocimiento del Espíritu Santo y su Naturaleza Transformadora.

Alcanzando Tu Destino en Dios

Spine: Enfoca tu Mente en las Cosas Más Allá del Sol — ERIC D. COOPER

Front cover

ENFOCA TU MENTE EN LAS COSAS

MÁS ALLÁ DEL SOL

Cómo desarrollar una Mentalidad del Reino

ERIC D. COOPER

Traducido por Briant Guzmán

Cover 2 — Estoy Enojado Con El Infierno

Back cover

Revelando las verdades de la guerra espiritual y el empoderamiento personal

¿Se siente abrumado por los ataques espirituales o aturdido por las grandes pérdidas infligidas por el maligno? "Estoy enojado con el infierno, ya no lo soportaré más" ofrece un rayo de esperanza y empoderamiento específicamente para usted.

El autor Eric Cooper expone sin miedo los planes insidiosos del enemigo, revelando cómo el diablo busca robar, matar y destruir los destinos de los creyentes en Cristo. Pero este libro es más que una simple exposición; es un manifiesto de guerra espiritual y empoderamiento personal, diseñado para ayudarte a recuperar tu victoria.

En su interior descubrirás:

- Perspectivas sobre la guerra espiritual: obtenga una comprensión más profunda de las tácticas del enemigo y cómo combatirlas con sabiduría bíblica.
- Estrategias prácticas para la victoria: aprenda siete consejos esenciales arraigados en las Escrituras para ayudarle a desarrollar un carácter piadoso y superar los desafíos de la vida.
- Testimonios de Triunfo: historias inspiradoras de personas que enfrentaron la adversidad de frente y salieron victoriosos a través del poder de la fe.

Eric Cooper es un líder, mentor y maestro profético apasionado por ayudar a las personas a descubrir su propósito en Cristo. Con más de cuatro décadas de experiencia, el estilo de liderazgo de Eric combina de manera única sabiduría, visión profética, gracia y compasión.

Spine: ESTOY ENOJADO CON EL INFIERNO — NO VOY A SOPORTARLO MÁS — ERIC D. COOPER

Front cover

ERIC D COOPER

ESTOY ENOJADO CON EL INFIERNO

NO VOY A SOPORTARLO MÁS

Revelando las verdades de la guerra espiritual y el empoderamiento personal

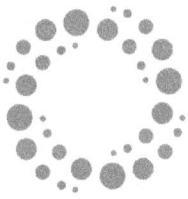

ERIC COOPER